MAIKA C. H
www.totalsensorywellness.com

TOTAL NUTRITION KITCHEN MAKEOVER™

How your kitchen
can help save your life!

Your kitchen could be making you fat, lethargic, and sick.
This easy handbook can show you how to:

Get past diet trends
Teach you the fundamentals of wholesome and toxic free nutrition
Show you how to create quick and healthy meals without slaving
Turn your kitchen into the quintessence of wellness
Give you the answer to permanent weight loss, energy, and vitality
Create A Kitchen That Cook's For You!

TOTAL NUTRITION KITCHEN MAKEOVER™
How your kitchen can help save your life!

Is your kitchen making you fat, lethargic, and sick?
This easy handbook can teach you how to get past diet trends and dogmas and help you understand the fundamentals of good, wholesome and toxin free nutrition. Have fun creating quick and healthy meals without slaving. Make your kitchen the heart of your home, the quintessence of wellness, and the answer to permanent weight loss, energy, and vitality.

Maika C. Henry Northrop, ND, CHT

Maika C. Henry Northrop is the owner and operator of Total Sensory Wellness Center, a holistic facility that helps people cultivate healthy lifestyles through the use of complimentary and alternative medicine. A cutting-edge approach to health care and prevention, Maika's franchised operation has a unique concept that is based on a membership program that makes her services affordable to the average individual. Maika has her B.S. in Alternative Medicine, and she is a Naturopathic Doctor, certified Colon Hydrotherapist, Bodywork Specialist, and Energy Practitioner.

Published by: Lulu, Inc.

First Edition: August 2006

Printed by: Lulu, Inc.

Cover Design by: Boutique Grafica, Inc.

Library of Congress Cataloging-in-Publication Data

Total Nutrition Kitchen Makeover™ is intended solely for informational and educational purposes and not as personal medical advice. Please consult your health care professional if you have any questions about your health.

ISBN-13 978-1-4243-2765-2

Maika C. Henry Northrop, ND
www.totalsensorywellness.com

TOTAL NUTRITION KITCHEN MAKEOVER™

How your kitchen can help
save your life!

"If you are planning for a year, sow rice; if you are planning for a decade, plant trees; if you are planning for a lifetime, educate people."
(Chinese Proverb)

Overall, I enjoyed reading the book and commend you on your willingness to teach others, using language that everyone can understand. What I appreciated most about the book, in addition to the content, was that you did not overcomplicate things and kept it simple.
~Dawn Chism

Ms. Henry has developed a handbook that reflects the approach she uses at Total Sensory Wellness Center. This handbook is gentle, informative, and truthful. There are no overnight solutions. What she does give you are practical tools and concepts that will lead you on your journey to a healthier, happier you. If you are a novice, experienced, or somewhere in the middle, this book has something for everyone. TNKM not only gives you a list of healthy kitchen appliances but also yummy recipes to use in the appliances. The chapters on herbs, fruits, and vegetables are comprehensive and can be used as your generic shopping list at the grocery store. The truth is our health is largely in our hands and this is a great aid for each of our personal journeys.
~Lawanda Butler

Your information content is very comprehensive and detailed. I love the charts and lists. They provide a good and quick reference!
~Stephanie Eugene

CONTENTS

Introduction 6

Chapter 1 - The Misleading Concept of Dieting 9

Chapter 2 - Diet Trends and Beliefs 15

Chapter 3 - Creating A Kitchen that Cook's For You 23

Chapter 4 - So I Have a Cooking Phobia, What's the Big Deal? 37

Chapter 5 - The Untapped Power of Women in the Kitchen 45

Chapter 6 - The Modern Lifestyle and Food 49

Chapter 7 - Re-discovering Wholesome and Natural Food 55

Chapter 8 - How to Get Most of your Nutrition from these Super Foods ... 65

Chapter 9 - Liberating Yourself from Sugar Addiction 75

Chapter 10 - How to Read Food Labels 81

Chapter 11 - Extending the Shelf Life of Perishable Foods 85

Chapter 12 - Herbs, Herbs and More Herbs 93

Chapter 13 - Going Organic 103

Chapter 14 - Let's Go Shopping: Everything You Need to Get Started Now! ... 131

Chapter 15 - The Wellness Kitchen; Cooking for Health and Weight Loss ... 137

Chapter 16 - Author's Closing Statement 147

Chapter 17 - Smart & Healthy Kitchen Recipes for Life 151

Source Section 174

Medical Disclaimer 177

INTRODUCTION

All of us are in a rush today. It is nearly impossible for people these days to step outside of themselves to observe whether the rush-induced way of living is good for them or not. Impossible I say, because most people are too preoccupied with life and all of the activities that inevitably fill up their space. We lose time and ourselves within it.

What is time? Time is considered a resource; a continuum of experience(s) that is mostly under our control and sufficient to accomplish anything. Nevertheless, time appears to elude folk these days. The modern-day pretext for eating wrong goes a little something like this: I don't have time to prepare wholesome meals because I have to take my son to Little League, or I don't cook because I'm a modern and liberated woman who has transcended the patriarchal definition of womanhood, or I spend too much time commuting and by the time I get home it's too late to cook, therefore eating out is a time-saver.

For many homemakers, the kitchen, which used to be the center of the home, has become almost a place to be dreaded. The kitchen is the "spirit" and "pulse" of the home. It is the place where meals are prepared and served. It is the place where people congregate and share their stories. It is the foundation of a good home that has the potential to bring forth good health and sometimes even good therapy. The kitchen evokes creativity and resourcefulness, and when a recipe goes awry, it can even offer invaluable lessons.

The most important aspect of the kitchen is that it is the highest expression of love and wellness. When your kitchen is set up correctly and is grounded in the basic principles of good health and nutrition, it can be a joyful place. Your kitchen can be a place where your family will receive the vital nutrients necessary to develop a healthy, energetic, and happy body.

In this handbook, you will explore the essential contents of a healthy kitchen's pantry. You will learn how to stock your refrigerator with wholesome real foods and discover a simple system that helps to extend the shelf life of your produce. I have included recipes that use these basic health-inducing ingredients. Learn about the history of tea and the fascinating ceremonies that have been the foundation of health for centuries. Learn how to start a tea tradition in your own household without opposition from family members. Learn about herbs and ingredients that keep your family slim and healthy or that trigger weight loss.

You'll even re-discover the healing and soothing benefits of soup. Mostly everyone enjoys soup and the wealth of comfort and curative properties it supplies the body when it is sick with a cold or the flu. Soup is easy to digest, fills you up fast, has very few calories, is packed with nutrients, and has various healing properties. Learn how to prepare soups effortlessly, without spending any more than 10 minutes in the kitchen! Best of all, your soup can be ready and waiting for you upon arrival from work, shopping, or running errands.

"Do you have a kinder, more adaptable friend in the food world than soup? Who soothes you when you are ill? Who refuses to leave you when you are impoverished and stretches its resources to give a hearty sustenance and cheer? Who warms you in the winter and cools you in the summer? Yet who also is capable of doing honor to your richest table and impressing your most demanding guests? Soup does its loyal best, no matter what undignified conditions are imposed upon it. You don't catch steak hanging around when you're poor and sick, do you?"
Judith Martin

This modern-day handbook is the result of the sheer determination of my clients at the Total Sensory Wellness Center in Waldorf, MD. I thank you for your support and your faith in my work. You have shown that all things are possible when you put forth the effort and are steadfast on your journey towards wholeness.

CHAPTER 1

THE FALLACY OF DIETING

The average American adult spends a large portion of his or her life dieting. The barrage of images on television, billboard ads, online, and in magazines bombards people daily with abnormal ideas of health and beauty. Truthfully, most people do not have the foggiest clue what "diet" means. Diet defined according to Webster's Dictionary is the usual food and drink of a person or animal.

Your diet, or the types of food and drink you consume daily, goes a long way in determining your health conditions. A regular habit of eating foods with inadequate nutritional value leads to a deteriorating quality of life. Your irregular food routines can devastate your body, making it sluggish, lethargic, toxic, and ultimately diseased.

Diet, or what you digest regularly for sustenance, can improve the overall health and functioning of the body. Some diets can heal the body of chronic and degenerative conditions while others can improve athletic performance. For instance, it is a proven fact that green tea contains antioxidant chemicals known as polyphenols that contain high levels of Vitamin E and Vitamin C. Another common fact that has been proven repeatedly through clinical studies is that garlic and onions contain chemicals that help limit the production of cancer-causing chemicals. These chemicals have been shown to have beneficial effects against several certain forms of cancer, including cancer of the stomach, colon, prostate, lungs, and mammary glands. Another in the long line of healing foods includes a mixture of lemon and olive oil to prevent gallstone attacks.

Now, we understand and agree that "diet" is the eating habits we practice. So, why are we hammered over the heads every day with false information and advertisements about diet and weight loss, all claiming to be healthy? And what is the actual truth?

America is quickly becoming the nation with the largest number of obese people in the world. Grocery store aisles are filled with instant meals and hundreds of quick snack choices to munch on at our workstations. As we continue to eat wrong and add weight, we dream of looking like the celebrities on television. We associate health with being celebrity thin and not with what we eat and how often we engage in physical activity. We have only ourselves to blame for the demand we created for weight-loss products. Even though we have faster computers, faster cars, and increasingly more efficient and faster technology, we have less time available in our lives. We want quick and easy fixes and gravitate to catchy phrases that pledge wondrous changes to our bodies with little effort. Americans end up consuming tons of diet pills, most of which are not just worthless, but actually harm us. The only persons they benefit are their manufacturers.

Businesses survive on money. Fatter Americans means bigger payouts for corporations when we rush to buy weight-loss products. Thus, it makes business sense for corporations to push unhealthy eating habits on the one hand and useless diet pills on the other hand. Moreover, to do this, they resort to a variety of fiction. In today's information age, statistics, opinions, and theories about nutrition are falling from the sky. If one hit you over the head, most of us would not know if it were fact, fiction, or gossip. Freedom of speech is a great right of the American people. Unfortunately, this freedom is easily abused. Because anyone has the freedom to say anything he or she pleases therefore misinformation circulates, just as freely, throughout the general public. An article or advertisement promoting a miracle pill may deliberately mislead, unknowingly misinform, or be a blatant lie. We may not know it until after buying the product, when we are being rushed to the hospital for medical complications, allergic reactions, or simply never benefiting at all.

Freedom of speech allows people to claim any benefit regarding their product. I bet if you had taken the time to review the product label, you may have avoided a trip to the hospital. In fact, many claims that appear to be true can often mislead people and eventually harm them. Do you remember Continental Baking Co.'s bread 'Fresh Horizons'? The company claimed that their bread had 40% fewer calories and 400 times more fiber than white bread because it contained alpha cellulose. It turned out that alpha cellulose was wood pulp, causing the revered comedian Johnny Carson to wonder how many loaves a person should eat to become eligible for environmental protection as a tree.

Sifting through the garbage to find the truth is not easy. First, go with your gut. Does losing a hundred pounds in two days sound like it will put my body at risk? Do I know what this miracle pill is made of? I would ask my doctor about it, but I know he will say it is not a good idea and tell me to exercise and re-consider my "diet?" There goes that "diet" word again. So you thought you were dieting when you took that pill. Guess again.

The miracle cure offered in the next big ad campaign does not consider individual lifestyles. A diabetic who eats carbohydrates that breaks down into sugar, constantly eating candy, and sugar will increase the dangers of his or her condition. A pill cannot substitute lifestyle practices. That is why diabetics are also advised to change their "diet" as well as engage in regular physical activity. Is the fear of losing a limb frightening enough to watch what you eat?

People working high-stress jobs can reduce their risk of heart attacks and other serious stress-related conditions by choosing the right "diet." Similarly, children who are sedentary can also benefit from the right diet. Of course, nutritious food is no substitute for lack of physical activity, given that it is also a very important aspect of health. But considering the possibility of reducing health risks is reason enough to take control of your diet today.

A single meal or one day of eating rich foods will not make or break an otherwise healthy eating pattern. What you eat on a regular daily basis is what matters the most. Enjoy your occasional indulgences, but follow a healthy meal plan most of the time.

The next question is: where can I find out what I truly need? There are somewhat reliable sources of information about nutrition that use standards of proof required by scientific research. Nutrition recommendations made to the public, such as the Dietary Guidelines for Americans and the Dietary Reference Intakes, are based on the consensus of scientific opinion. Nevertheless, do remember that a scientific opinion is an educated judgment that is not founded on proof of certainty, although some scientific research may be used as support.

Even science has its flaws. How often has science refuted a claim that was until recently considered- "scientific" fact? Life is a continuous process of trial and error. However, some fundamentals about nutrition do not change, and they will be discussed at greater length in subsequent chapters.

Everyone has specific dietary needs. There is no one specific diet that can address the vast and varied dietary needs of individuals, all of who have differences in lifestyle, genetic makeup, and activity. The best site to access information for your nutritional and dietary needs, information that is based on lifestyle, activity, gender, pregnancy, age, special needs, and conditions, etc. can be found at www.dietitians.ca. Dietitians of Canada provide consumers information and advice for healthy eating and food preparation. You can assess your nutrition profile, address nutrition challenges, and even build a one-day menu. This site is very comprehensive and can provide you with almost everything you need to know about diet and nutrition. The site will help you find the right foods to eat based on your current physiological state.

Be pragmatic about your body size and shape. Your genes have a lot to do with the way you look, so avoid trying to be someone you are not meant to be. Feeling good about yourself starts with accepting the way you look. Before judging your size harshly, remember, healthy bodies come in all shapes and sizes!

CHAPTER 2

DIET TRENDS AND BELIEFS

Today more than ever, people are becoming more confused about diets, nutrition, and the trends that the "weight loss" industry promotes. The Atkins Diet, South Beach Diet, Eat Right For Your Type, The Fat Flush Diet, Zone Diet, Negative Calorie Weight Loss Solution, Dash Diet, and the Diabetes Diet are just a few of the many diet plans available. With so many "quick fix" solutions available, it's no wonder many people find it difficult to make decisions about their diet.

Scientific evaluations show that some of these diets actually work for a short time. By taking in fewer calories for the first couple of weeks, you lose water and lean muscle. However, your goal was to drop the fat. When you deprive yourself of nutrients, you may get cranky and irritable more often on your quest for quick and easy weight loss. Two weeks after quitting the diet plan, you gain twice the weight back. Now you can expect dramatic mood swings from your new and frustrated personality.

It was inevitable, but now you've become a weight-loss yo-yo. In the long run, you will be unhappy with the results from the first product and the second product, and will be jumping on the bandwagon to the next great product advertised late at night on your way to the refrigerator to grab a snack. People at your office start to notice. They may not say anything to your face, but they are talking.

Most of these diets overemphasize the remarkable results of eating a single type of food. Alternatively, they bash it in your head to avoid a certain type of food altogether, such as carbohydrates. Robbing your body of other foods with valuable nourishment will leave you with an imbalance. The body needs an array of healthy foods. Have you ever heard of ketosis? It's a process that occurs in your body during starvation, due to lack of carbohydrates. Ketosis may cause constipation, nausea, vomiting, and fatigue. Long-term problems from ketosis may be heart disease, bone loss, and kidney damage.

Studies for low-carb or no-carb diets have shown weight loss after a year if you can follow the diet that long, but watch out for the complications caused by malnutrition. Don't open the door for illness and ailments. Raw food diets have its pros and cons. Some believe that cooking is necessary because vital ingredients and vitamins in certain foods are not activated until the foods are cooked. There is no scientific proof that nutrients are "activated" through the cooking process; some research studies have shown that cooked (especially fried) foods actually activate T-cell activity and deplete the body of vital enzymes necessary in the metabolic process. There are various types of Raw Foodists however, and the Fruitarian seems to be the most malnourished. Many people with chronic and degenerative conditions, cancer, and inflammatory conditions have managed to take control of their health following a raw food diet.

Again, certain foods can be very beneficial when the condition calls for it. A diet must serve a specific purpose, and you must consider your lifestyle to determine which diet will ultimately work best for you. Bear in mind that diets have a tendency to change over time as your environment changes, your level of activity may increase or decrease, or you may decide to conceive a child. Always consider these variables when making food choices.

Be cautious of diets that promote their own products as the secret to a beautiful and healthy body. Seriously consider it. If a brand name tells you to only use their products, attend their seminars, buy from their affiliates or you will fail your weight loss goal, does that appear to be a marketing strategy for developing customer loyalty and generate more sales? There are also many companies that are multi-level marketing groups in disguise. These groups ultimately try to encourage you to become a distributor of their product by bombarding you with sales tactics, kits, and monetary incentives.

At times, you'll come across a few reputable organizations that sell pharmaceutical-grade herbs and/or supplements that are very effective at helping one attain their weight-loss objectives, coupled with a sound and reasonable diet. The key is to use these products as tools or compliments to accomplishing your weight-reduction goals. The problem with these products is that people tend to go to extremes; losing sight of the overall objective can make a person fall prey to false advertisement. Again, the objective should be to cultivate a healthy approach to dieting, making choices that support wellness, i.e. reading food labels, buying organic versus conventional produce, eating smaller portions, drinking more water and less caffeinated or carbonated beverages, exercising, and effectively managing stress.

We have all seen the before and after weight-loss pictures. Sally was four hundred pounds in the first slide. In the second, she is only one hundred pounds and has the same hair color, but the faces don't match. Was that really Sally in both pictures? Ask some of your friends if they know anyone who has tried that diet. Did they see dramatic results? Have they had any health problems? Ask yourself is it worth your life being the first person you know to try that miracle pill?

Pay attention to scientists who star in commercials. Remember, that person was paid to be in that promotion. Does he or she really believe in what they are selling and saying? How can you be sure? Most likely, they are actors pretending to be scientists and doctors. Watch closely to some of the infomercials. There are some airing late at night that are selling completely different products but have some of the same actors telling you how well a product, service, or "get-rich" quick scheme worked for them. Either that person loves trying products on infomercials or he is an actor, who more than one casting director believed had an honest face.

Some of these commercials are shot directly in the call centers that sell these products. They pick employees from the sales floor to star in the commercials or sit in the audience to ask pre-arranged questions. These same employees will be the ones reading the sales scripts to you when you call in to get more information on the miracle cure to your weight problems with the one goal to get your credit card number before you hang up.

What about weight-loss surgery for obesity such as gastric bypass, stomach stapling, lap banding, or liposuction? In cases of morbid obesity (this means life or death), then these types of surgical procedures can be a godsend. However, there are far more effective, less risky and permanent solutions to weight loss than these invasive and sometimes fatal procedures. Again, the key is to change the source of your sustenance—the kitchen—and you can improve your health dramatically. Remember that many surgeons underestimate the risks that are involved in these so-called quick-fix solutions and often skirt over the issue. Following is a list of complications that can be expected:

- Up to 20% of patients suffer surgical complications, and 1.9% actually dies within 30 days of the operation. Complications can be many, from infections to perforations, leaking stomach acids, to abdominal hernias.

- Subsequent to surgery, the rapid weight loss increases the risk of gallstones.

- Risk of vomiting as is found in stomach stapling if a patient doesn't adapt their meal sizes to their reduced stomach capacity, which is often substantially smaller than a portion.

TOTAL NUTRITION KITCHEN MAKEOVER™

- In liposuction, the body often regenerates the removed fat cells and the weight will be regained.

- Spleen injury, which often leads to the removal in about 0.3% of patients to control operative bleeding.

- Abdominal surgery can cause dense scar tissue

- Leaks from staple line breakdown

- Marginal ulcers and stenosis of the spine

The road to long-term health is not an easy road to travel, but it certainly makes the journey more enjoyable. Most people who opt for these invasive treatments are not considered morbidly obese. In fact, many of them do it to quickly get rid of stubborn pockets of fat. Regular exercise, a healthy whole-grain-based diet, effective stress management, and consistency are ultimately the answer to permanent weight loss. C'mon, it's really not rocket science.

Again, diet is the practice or routine you keep with the foods you eat to sustain a comfortable and healthy life. Save your money and exercise self-control. You hold the key to creating a better you. Simply remember a few things:

- Watch your liquids. Replace sodas or fruit juices that are filled with unhealthy sugars with eating actual fruit and drinking water. If you want to add flavor to your water, slice up the fruit (most people prefer lemon as it is much more practical and quickly infuses your water with flavor and electrolytes) and put it into your water.

- Add fruits and vegetables to your regular eating routine. If you already eat one fruit a day, increase it to two. It's best to eat your fruits in the morning, the time your brain needs the sugar the most. Eat loads of vegetables for the remaining day as it nourishes, alkalizes, and builds a strong healthy body. Gradually building up your healthy eating standards is easier than quitting cold turkey.

- Watch your portion sizes. We eat larger and larger portions thanks to the fast food corporations getting us customized to super-sizing.

- Choose organic whole grain breads (many people are developing allergies to wheat gluten; consider buckwheat as an alternative since it doesn't have gluten in it; it's light, tastes great and is loaded with fiber), whole grain pastas, and brown rice as alternatives to the simple carbohydrates (i.e. white sugar, white bread, white rice, regular pasta) that are known for causing health problems.

The following worksheets will help you make the right diet choice based on your current lifestyle and condition. Of course, you will need to make the food choices yourself, but it will help you narrow things down a bit and guide you in the right direction. It's a good idea to make several copies and hand one to each family member, children alike. The old adage "give a man a fish, you feed him for a day, teach him how to fish and you feed him for a lifetime" is very much applicable in this case. Empower and teach your family, your friends, your co-workers, and your neighbors and you'll notice how easy it becomes to make this change a permanent part of your life. Don't forget to take it with you when shopping at the grocery store; you'll find shopping a whole lot easier with this handy tool at your disposal.

Grain Products	Vegetables and Fruit	Milk & Dairy Products	Meat and Alternatives	Fats, Oils, and Sweets
Grain products are good for you as they are good sources of vitamins and minerals, carbohydrates like starch and fiber. Whole-grain foods have more fiber than white grain foods. There are many kinds of whole-grain foods to choose from as follows: - Oatmeal - Brown rice - Grits - Barley - Quinoa - Millet	Fresh and organic fruits and vegetables are low in fat, calories and sodium and rich in nutrients. If you buy frozen vegetables with special sauces, you may also be adding fat and calories unconsciously. Buy frozen vegetables without special sauces and acquire the same nutrients as fresh vegetables. Fruits are important sources of vitamins and carbohydrates. They are naturally low in calories and sweet. In addition, they are good sources of water. Choose from:	Milk, yogurt, and cheese are important because all the nutrients work together to keep our bones strong and healthy. Choose From: - Low-fat organic milk (cow or goat) - Low-fat cheese from healthy cows, goats or sheep (preferably unpasteurized cheese) - Kefir - Plain & low-fat organic yogurt may add fresh fruit - Fresh organic whole eggs from free range	Some meats and meat products are high in fat. To remove this extra fat, you can choose leaner cuts like chuck, bottom round, or top round of beef. Because eggs are a good source of iron and protein, they are also counted as a meat serving. Most of the fat in eggs is found in the yolk; use the egg whites if using as a protein substitute. - Free Range Poultry - Beef from Pasteur fed cows (choose lean cuts) - Choose Deep	Fats and oils like salad dressings, mayonnaise, butter, margarine, and lard are high in calories due to the level of fat they contain. For example, most margarines contain trans fats, which cannot be digested and therefore is automatically stored in the fat cells. The main ingredient of sweets like candy, soft drinks, syrups, jams, and jellies is sugar. Good sources of fats, oils and sugars are: **Monounsaturated Fats and Oils** - Olive Oil - Ghee - Canola Oil

	Fruits	chicken	ocean fish that have the lowest mercury level such as:	- Peanut Oil
- Buckwheat	- Apples			- Flax Oil
- Bulgur	- Oranges	- Low-fat cottage cheese		- Walnuts
	- Grapes			- Cashew
- Cracked or Whole Wheat Bread	- Melons			- Almonds and most nuts
	- Cherries	- Ghee (natural & kosher butter substitute)	- Halibut	- Avocados
	- Pineapple			
	- Kiwi		- Spanish Mackerel	
- Whole Grain Pasta	- Grapefruit	- Whey	- Trout (fresh water)	**Sugars**
	- Mango			- Agave (Great for Diabetics & low on the Glycemic Index)
	- Apricot		- Perch (fresh water)	
- Wild Rice	- Plums			
	- Pears			
- Bran Cereal	- Peaches		- Wild Alaskan Sockeye Salmon	- Honey
	- Pomegranate			
- Amaranth	- Bananas			
	- Blueberries		- Tilapia	- Maple Syrup
	- Wild Berries			
	- Papaya		- Catfish	- Stevia
	Vegetables		- Snapper	- Raw Cane Sugar
	- Broccoli			
	- Asparagus		- Lobster	*stay away from all artificial sweeteners to include splenda which is a poisonous chlorocarbon (simply chlorinated sugar)
	- Carrots			
	- Peppers			
	- Cabbages			
	- Eggplant			
	- Brussels Sprouts			
	- Red Onions			
	- Celery			
	- Lettuces			
	- Fresh Corn			
	- String Beans			
	- Squash			
	- Cucumbers			
	- Potatoes			
	- Sweet Potatoes			
	- Turnips			
	- Greens including Kale, Collard, Spinach & Mustard			

Ultimately, the way you transcend diet trends and beliefs is by wearing the skeptic's hat when shopping for your food. Question everything and read your food labels. Your body is like the Taj Mahal, a sacred temple. Would you adorn this temple with furnishing from Wal-Mart or would you make sure it has the finest, imported furniture hand-crafted by expert artisans. Your body only produces as good as the fuel it is supplied; garbage in, garbage out. Supply your body with good, non-genetically modified preservative and artificial free ingredients, and watch your energy levels rise, your mind become sharper, and your overall performance improve. It's really not rocket science; we tend to make things more complicated than they have to be.

CHAPTER 3

CREATING A KITCHEN THAT COOKS FOR YOU

The modern kitchen has a few gadgets and gizmos that can help reduce time in the kitchen and afford more time for other activities. Of course, that's what modern America is all about. Unfortunately, most of us are spending little to no time in the kitchen and surrendering our health to fast food pirates.

It's hard to go into the kitchen and cook a meal when time is limited and you are exhausted from work or chasing after a child all day. We can come up with all kinds of excuses why there isn't time to cook. Funny, isn't it, how we will sit on the couch and stare at the television for an hour when we have so much to do but won't step foot in the kitchen to cook? There are many nourishing meals you can cook in thirty minutes. It's a matter of getting you motivated to go into the kitchen for more than just a snack cake.
In order to seize the day, you must first begin by seizing your refrigerator, your kitchen cabinets, and your appliances. Ask yourself, is my kitchen designed to promote health and wellness or is it designed to promote sickness and emotional eating dependencies?

Your kitchen is the heart of your home. If you are afraid of your kitchen or continue to come up with solutions to stay out of your kitchen, then the rest of the elements of your life are not being pumped with essential nutrients to sustain them. A healthier you can achieve more of the goals you set for yourself. If you are not setting goals for yourself, maybe it's because you don't have the energy or the drive.

A well-organized kitchen can help reduce stress and create quality time with your family and decrease preparation time for meals. If you can start improving your health by organizing your kitchen, would you turn that down? Organizing your kitchen can do more than improve your health. The kitchen is a place we entertain most of our guests. An organized and healthy kitchen offers a better atmosphere for your visiting family, neighbors, and friends.

The first step is to clean out the clutter. Get rid of everything in your cupboard that has been there a while. Throw out half-empty boxes that have been lingering around for months. Trash all the stuff you stored at the bottom of the cupboard because you had nowhere else to put them. Do the same thing for the refrigerator, then the cabinets, and then the drawers. Take an inventory of all the things you throw out. These are items you and your family never use. Save money and avoid buying these items again.

Next, take everything off the countertops. Disinfect them with green cleaning products, products safe for the environment. When you rearrange them, place the items you use the most in a triangle formation from the stove and the refrigerator. You should be able to access appliances on either side of the stove, and then turn back to the refrigerator for additional ingredients with ease. Easier access to these items will make cooking a littler easier for you.

Now that the kitchen is clean, design a plan for its use. Plan in advance what you are going to cook. Make a list of all your favorite foods. Get the children involved and have them write down their favorite foods. Once they're done, scratch off the ice cream and cookies. Organize the meals you and your family have written down into categories. Have a category for meals that will take around thirty minutes to prepare and cook. Then, have a separate category for meals that take longer, an hour or more.

Place a magnetized memo board on your refrigerator, and write down the short prep meals that you will cook during the week when you have less time. On the days the family has more time together, typically the weekend, write in the longer prep and cook or prepare the meals as a family. The more your family supports your desire to get them healthier, the easier the journey will be.

For the shorter meals, on the night before or on the day before you go off to work, defrost the meats by transferring them from the freezer to the refrigerator. Set any ingredients you will need aside in a designated area in the refrigerator. Chop all of your vegetables and place them in a Ziplock bag, infuse them with herbs, spices, and olive oil. The following morning before you head off to work, half the prep time has been cut down and all you have to do is put the food in the automatic pots and let it cook.

What's an automatic pot, you might ask? An automatic pot is a Crock-Pot, a rice cooker, or any kitchen appliance that is designed to make cooking fun, easy, and convenient, and most notably, some are equipped with timers, so you can set it and forget it. Say goodbye to being a slave to your kitchen once and for all! At the risk of sounding like a commercial, when you have these modern, state-of-the-art, and yes, affordable appliances in your kitchen, you have freedom.

Wouldn't it be nice to come home every day to the smell of homemade food as if you had your own personal chef cooking in your kitchen?

So you're on your way to work and you've invested in your automatic pots that have built-in timers set to come on or off at will. You remove your defrosted meats from the refrigerator, you add your favorite herbs and spices, and set it in your Crock-Pot (which by the way acts as a roaster oven when no water is added). You then proceed to place your brown rice in the rice cooker, and add water and sea salt. Most automatic rice cookers with timers have vegetable steamers on top, so while the rice is boiling the steam cooks the vegetables. Go right ahead, take your marinated vegetables and dump them in the vegetable tray. Now set it and forget it!

Here is a list of must-have kitchen appliances and tools:

- 2 electric Crock-Pots with programmable built-in timers
- 1 rice cooker with programmable built-in timer
- The George Forman Grill
- Toaster oven with programmable built-in timer
- Vita-Mix juicer
- Hand food chopper
- Large 15" Round Natural Stoneware Clay
- Japanese vegetable knife
- Silicone garlic peeler
- Electric pressure-cooker with programmable built-in timer
- Juicer
- Harsch fermenting pot
- Mortar and pestle
- Salad spinner
- Mason jars (all sizes)
- Hand held Food Saver appliance
- Non-stick Professional Excalibur cookware
- ResherLonger Miracle Food Storage

OK so you have to make a small investment up front, but in return you've reduced the stress of coming up with quick dinner ideas. You also saved yourself money by cutting out the fast food bill. And believe me, once you start preparing and eating your own home-cooked meals, you won't want to eat out. Grocery shopping will be much easier, and you will have a list already made out for you. Grocery trips will take less time. What are you going to do with that extra time saved? Exercise, maybe?

Anyway, let's talk about the tools of the kitchen and why they are necessary if you want to manage your time and lead a "normal" and "healthy" life filled with exuberant energy.

Electric Crock-Pot with programmable built-in timers
Crock-Pots and slow-cookers are very convenient appliances. In fact, it is estimated that 8 out of 10 households have one either collecting dust on a pantry shelf or taking full advantage of its practical benefits. Just put your ingredients into the slow-cooker in the morning and you can enjoy a delicious home-cooked meal by dinnertime.

In addition to being convenient and timesaving, the process of slow-cooking allows flavors to blend and spices to meld. It also has the ability to hold in moisture and vitamins and decrease the number of pots you have to clean at the end of the meal.

The idea of your next meal simmering away for six to ten hours may seem kind of strange, but consider some of the advantages: An eight- to ten-hour Crock-Pot recipe uses less than 25 cents worth of electricity; you could wake to a warm, creamy pot of cereal tomorrow morning; the kitchen stays cool in summer; your stove or oven has more space available for big holiday or party meals; crocks are great for keeping food warm at potlucks or on buffets; and, maybe most importantly, there is only one pot to clean after dinner!

There are quite a few slow-cooker recipe books on the market and several websites dedicated to them as well. Overall, using a slow-cooker can be as easy as 1-2-3 and can be adapted to meet your specific dietary and lifestyle needs. Here are a few tips to help you get started:

- To convert your favorite recipes, try this formula: one hour at a stovetop simmer or in a 350°F oven equals eight hours in the slow-cooker on low or about four hours on high.

- Don't peek! Every time you lift the lid, you need to add 20-30 minutes to the total cooking time.

- Reduce added liquids by 25-30%. One cup is plenty for most recipes other than soups. Slow-cookers do not allow moisture to evaporate like other methods, so for some things you may want less than a cup of liquid.

- Always thaw frozen ingredients before adding to cooker.

- Prepare your recipe the night before and refrigerate right in the ceramic container. To be safe, refrigerate any meat ingredient in a separate container. In the morning, start up the cooker and add an extra hour to allow for the chill to wear off. (This also buys you extra time if more than eight hours will pass before your meal.)

- Read the manufacturer's instructions. Most cookers should be filled at least halfway, but if more than 2/3 full, you run the risk of a messy boil-over.

- Whole spices and herbs hold their flavors best. If you use ground or crushed, increase the quantity or add near the end of cooking time. Fresh herbs should always be added at the end of cooking to preserve their flavor.

Rice cooker with programmable built-in timer

The cooking of rice has been a tricky process that requires perfect timing, and errors can result in inedible rice. Rice cookers aim to avoid these problems by controlling heat and timing while cooking rice. Although the rice cooker doesn't necessarily speed up the cooking process, the cook's involvement in cooking rice with a rice cooker is drastically reduced and simplified.

Rice cookers are typically used for the preparation of plain or lightly seasoned rice. I like to toss peas in my rice cooker to add some variety to my rice dishes. If you have a rice cooker designed with a basket above the rice, it can also be used as a vegetable steamer. Rice cookers are simple to use; just add the measured amount of rice, seasoning, and cold water. Close the lid and activate the cooking cycle.

The George Forman Grill

George Foreman entered the food appliance business and launched the George Foreman Lean Mean **Fat-Reducing Grilling Machine** that has become very popular around the world with its clamshell design. Like other similar grills, the George Foreman grill is structured to drain fat for healthier cooking. The grill can be used for grilling chicken, turkey breasts, salmon or tuna steaks, and other boneless meats while at the same time it can be used for grilling or cooking Panini, sandwiches and quesadillas. The grill features a clamshell design with

Teflon-coated heating surfaces. The slanted grated bottom surface allows for easy drainage of fat and other coagulants. You can have a juicy, low-fat slab of grilled meat ready to be consumed in less than five minutes. How's that for fast food!

Toaster oven with programmable built –in timer
A toaster oven is much like an oven, only smaller with one door and a tray within. It is great for baking, broiling, and toasting, and it is also easy to clean. Toaster ovens are excellent when it comes to making casseroles and roasting vegetables. When you purchase one that has an automatic turn on/off timer, you have the convenience of spending less time in the kitchen. For example, if you plan to make a casserole dish for dinner, all that is necessary is that you toss all of your ingredients in your ovenware, place it in the oven, set the timer to turn on and off at a certain time, then go about your business. When you come home, your meal is completely ready and all that's left to do is set the table, say your blessings, and eat as a family.

Vita-Mix juicer
Vita-Mix juicer, contrary to its name, is not a juicer. The Vita-Mix juicer is the only machine in the market that breaks down cell walls to deliver the full benefit of nutrients; and in doing so; it makes nutritional supplements almost unnecessary. Research studies suggest that certain foods are true cancer-fighting warriors. Raw and organic nuts, seeds, berries, vegetables, and fruits can easily blend in your Vita-Mix juicer and create a highly concentrated and nutritious meal.

The best way to get enough of these powerful cancer fighters into your system every day is by using the Vita-mix juicer daily. Unlike the other juicers out there, the Vitamix doesn't separate the healthful pulp from the liquid in the fruit/vegetable. It literally pulverizes the food effectively and efficiently. It's also easier to use and clean and is more versatile than any other juicer on the market.

Vita-Mix makes eating nine servings of fruits and vegetables every day amazingly easy. Just drop whole foods-seeds, stems and all into your Vita-Mix, flip the switch, and you get delicious whole food juices, smoothies, soups, and frozen treats in a matter of minutes with the enzymes in tact.

The real bonus is that you are also getting up to three times more nutrition than you get from eating those same foods cooked or raw. The Vita-Mix juicer can be used for a number of creative recipes such as whole food juice made from left over, overripe fruits! Puree fruits and vegetables for baby food without the irritation of additives or preservatives! Serve delicious sorbets, puddings, or smoothies at home for a portion of the cost! You can even create incredibly delicious ice cream sundaes.

Large 15" round natural stoneware clay
Natural stoneware clay is a godsend in the kitchen. The clay distributes heat efficiently for even baking and browning. I absolutely love mine as you can easily satisfy your fresh-baked pizza cravings with the large stone. The flat baking stones are available in three sizes: 13" diameter, 15" diameter, and the 12" x 15" Rectangle Stone to suit your needs. Your baking stone is ideal for baking and reheating food such as fresh or frozen pizzas, tortillas, biscuits, rolls or breadsticks, cookies, pretzels, and much more.

Stoneware is delicate, so always allow it to cool to room temperature before adding liquid or cleaning it. You also want to avoid dropping it or exposing it to extreme temperature changes. In addition, stoneware has a tendency to retain heat, which is wonderful for keeping your dish warm; however, it can cause burns when hot and handled improperly. Therefore, always use a heat-resistant oven mitt or pad for precaution.

Hand food chopper
A hand food chopper features a self-contained base that holds chopped foods after use, stainless-steel blades that easily chop vegetables, herbs, or fruit depending on your requirements, high-impact plastic construction that ensures durability and the chopper disassembles easily for quick hassle-free cleanup. I use my chopper for onions and just about any vegetable that takes time to chop, which can be quite tedious. In a matter of seconds, you can chop onions, garlic, and peppers without the tears. The food chopper is an absolute must for an anti-slave approach to cooking and preparing meals!

Japanese vegetable knife
The Nakiri bocho and usuba bocho are the most commonly used Japanese vegetable knives. These knives are thinner and have a straight blade that helps cut vegetables without the irritation of a horizontal push or pull. In the world of preparing meals and chopping vegetables, a good quality knife is the key to a successful journey in the kitchen. The Japanese vegetable knife

is unparallel when it comes to other cutting knives. The thin blade allows for easy cutting of vegetables.

The difference between a Nakiri bocho and usuba bocho lies in the fact that a usuba bocho is sharpened from only one side and allows for cutting of thinner slices. For your first knife, try looking for one that has a very slight curve along the sharpened edge. It's easier if there is a slight bow along the cutting edge. Although these knives can be purchased as stainless steel, always choose a metal that will rust like the softer carbon-steel metal. The carbon-steel metal sharpens much easier than its stainless steel counterpart.

Silicone garlic peeler

Garlic is strong smelling and tasty, and one simple yet effective tool makes cloves easier to skin, crush, chop, press, roast, and so on. No kitchen is complete without a garlic peeler that is developed for the exclusive purpose of extracting the awesome flavor of garlic.

Garlic is an essential component used in many recipes. Many people love the taste of garlic and cannot seem to get enough of it. For these, garlic can be added to recipes in bulk. Since garlic must be removed from its skin before it is used, several tools can assist in making this difficult job much easier.

This one particular garlic peeler will simply amaze you. Out of all the peelers on the market, this inexpensive tube of silicone rubber that strips the peel from garlic cloves by rolling it on the counter makes using garlic fun and easy. Whether a single garlic clove or a whole head of garlic is being used for a recipe, everyone can take advantage of this wonderfully simple garlic peeler. Everybody who has peeled individual garlic cloves using their fingernails knows how tiresome it can be. This garlic peeler can significantly speed up the peeling process and is very easy to use and most importantly clean. By rolling the tube on the garlic, the skin of the garlic sticks to the peeler and the inside of the garlic clove is left for cooking. Using this amazing tool will speed up the garlic peeling process and at the same time eliminate the everlasting garlic smell that remains on fingers.

Electric pressure-cooker with programmable built-in timer

Electric pressure-cookers are one of the best modern appliance improvements. If you want to create one of the best tasting stews, beans, and grains, you'll want to add this to your kitchen. These units are not only safe to use, but also the cooking time is shortened immensely and the increase in flavor is incredible. Some safety mechanisms on electric models for customer safety also add to making the electric pressure-cooker a good investment. These include a release dial with locking handle for added safety and convenience and a pop-up indicator to indicate when there is pressure in the cooker and drops when the pressure is released and high and low pressure settings. Your first pressure-cooker can be the last you will ever buy, so don't worry about the initial investment; it's worth every dollar you spend.

Juicer

A juicer is a machine that helps extract the juice of fruits, vegetables, leafy greens, and herbs. A juicer greatly differs from a blender, as a juicer separates the juice from the pulp. Juicers are available in two categories, a centrifugal juicer that separates the juice from the pulp and the masticating juicer that breaks down the fruit into a pulp before extracting the juice. Juicers are essential for every kitchen today. They are an excellent means of making quick and easy juices encouraging healthy eating.

Harsch fermenting pot

Fermented vegetables are important for healthy nutrition. Natural fermentation is one of the oldest means of preservation. Lactic acid bacteria subject the vegetables to a fermentation process. The vegetable becomes preserved, it develops a pleasantly sour taste, and it is rich in vitamins and minerals. They are an excellent source of enzymes, and healthy probiotics are easier to digest than raw or cooked vegetables and can enhance the nutrient value of any meal. Sally Fallon of the Weston A. Price foundation calls cultured vegetables "super foods" because they are partially digested, and the bioavailability of the nutrients requires very little digestion and adds to the enzyme stores of your body. Kefir, sour kraut, kim chee, cultured cream, buttermilk, cultured vegetables, etc. all add predigested food full of vitamins and minerals, normal flora, and enzymes back into the body.

These beautifully designed stoneware Crock-Pots produce liters of pickled vegetables very easily. Their use of ceramic weight stones purges mold while their clever water-sealing system allows fermentation gases to escape without allowing air to enter. Simple instructions for use and recipes are included with a new fermenting pot.

The Harsch fermenting pot comes with a 2-piece stone that is used to weigh down the lid and apply pressure during the fermentation process, so there is no need for you to use your own stones.

Mortar and pestle

A mortar and pestle are tools used together to grind and mix substances, usually spices. They were traditionally used in pharmacies to crush ingredients when making a prescription. The most common uses of a mortar and pestle today include making of ingredients such as guacamole and pesto sauce. They can also be used to grind spices, seeds, or nuts.

Salad spinner

A salad spinner is a plastic bowl with a removable plastic strainer and special top that, when closed and activated, spins the strainer. When the strainer is filled with freshly washed salad, the spinning motion pulls excess water from the salad.

Your salad should be as dry as possible prior to adding condiments to it, since oil and water do not mix. Salad spinners are the easiest way to dry your greens. To make things easier, the salad spinner comes with options such as wash/dry spinners where you can wash and spin-dry the greens in the same container. When storing salad greens, it is important to keep them wet, and the salad spinner canvas storage bag does just this. Simply wet the bag, wring it dry, place the leaves inside, and put the bag in the fridge.

Mason jars (all sizes)

The most well-known fruit jars in the industry are the mason jars. Previous jar-sealing methods included waxed paper, leather, or skin followed by cork stoppers and wax sealers. The breakthrough came with the development of the zinc cap for the shoulder-seal jar. The mason jar had a threaded neck that fit with the threads in a metal cap to screw down to the shoulder of the jar. Later, a top seal above the threads and under a glass lid was introduced. The screw cap pressed tightly against the inverted lid, with rubber seal underneath, thus creating an excellent seal. A type of this closure still is in use today, although augmented with various other closure designs. Mason jars are excellent for storing fruit, vegetables, dried goods, cooked foods, freshly made condiments, and liquids such as broth. They are available in all sizes to suit your storage needs.

Handheld food saver appliance

A handheld food saver appliance is a powerful and convenient appliance—a must for every kitchen. Its small, compact handheld design in no way reduces the power you would receive with a full-size food saver appliance. The "Easy Glide Nozzle" fits directly into jars and utensils without the use of a hose or attachment. A one-touch application allows for instant airtight vacuum—all with the simple press of a button that can easily seal your mason jars. What other better way to preserve your refrigerated food and keep your dried herbs, grains, seeds, and nuts fresh?

Non-stick Professional Excalibur cookware

Excalibur is the toughest, longest-lasting, most durable non-stick coating on the market. Why is Excalibur so much better than other non-sticks? Because it's reinforced with stainless steel. Most coatings are just what the word suggests: a coating applied over a metal substrate — a surface finish. Excalibur is a system. Stainless steel is arc-sprayed onto the article, actually becoming a part of it. The stainless-steel matrix is then impregnated with premium non-stick coatings. The result: a coating system with the toughness of stainless steel and the "release" properties of the best non-stick—the most durable coating system ever created. The Hard Anodized treatment process is a recent development to harden the surface of aluminum cookware. This process changes the molecular structure of the metal and creates a surface that is very hard and impervious to food acids. The pan itself retains the even heating and heat conductivity of aluminum, and best of all, it's guaranteed to last up to 25 years!

FresherLonger Miracle Food Storage

Finally, the creation of a storage container that ends the expense and frustration of tossing out costly food that has spoiled or grown moldy much too quickly has arrived! These awesome containers are infused with silver nanoparticles to retard the growth of microorganisms that cause spoilage. According to studies, FresherLonger has been shown to reduce the growth of bacteria by over 98% as compared to conventional containers. Best of all, it has an airtight gasket locking system, is odor impermeable, spill proof, shatterproof, and safe for dishwashers, microwaves and the fridge. Your nominal initial investment will give you a nice return for years to come! Say goodbye to spoiled or wasted food forever!

TOTAL NUTRITION KITCHEN MAKEOVER™

CHAPTER 4

SO I HAVE A COOKING PHOBIA... WHAT'S THE BIG DEAL?

What's the big deal? The big deal is you literally are what you eat. Cooking and preparing your meal is a big deal. It's a big deal because that is the course of your sustenance, the alpha and the omega of health, vitality, energy, and total life success.

Without good, wholesome, and nutritious food, how will you muster up the strength to wrestle with your active and growing child? How will you wake up in the morning full of energy and motivation to take on the world? How will you finish that college degree or be the first one to come up with the ingenious suggestion that will get you the promotion you've always wanted?

Have you ever stumbled out of bed in the morning and skipped breakfast? You skipped breakfast because of your kitchen phobia. If you did get breakfast, you picked it up on the way to work or after dropping the kids off to school. More than likely, it was fast food or some food or cereal bar. An advertising genius concocted a slogan just to get you to believe that the snack bar will replace all the nutrients a home-cooked meal can provide your body.

Because you did not properly fuel your body the night before, you woke up that following morning more famished than usual. Throughout the night, your body fasts naturally. It is during this time that the body repairs itself. The fast food you supplied it, however, did not provide your body with enough nutrients to do its job. And to add insult to injury, you continue to skip breakfast, despite how sleepy and lethargic you feel.

What do you do to boost your energy levels all day until lunchtime? Well, you start your morning off with a Starbucks Double Shot Espresso (the kind that comes in a can; you have a case in your refrigerator). Right around 10:00 am you start to feel sluggish again and decide to hit the snack machine. "A Snicker bar will do the trick," you tell yourself. There is no fruit or trail mix in your kitchen to pack for work. In fact, your refrigerator is bare. Instead, you snack on the contents of the vending machine. And every morning the cycle continues. Your body is becoming more sensitive to sugar and fats and ultimately you are putting yourself one step closer to more health complications.

Lunchtime arrives and the quick bursts that you received from the vending machine snack is over just as quickly as it started and now you are finally coming down. Your stomach may be full from the junk food, but your body is still going to tell your brain that you are hungry. Now, you are going to eat larger portions of food to compensate for what you didn't get the night before or at breakfast. You unwittingly double the calories that you take in

(It's a natural instinct to feast when one is famine). Your body has to now work overtime to digest all of this food. You now feel sleepy. And the sugar yo-yo saga continues.

It's obvious that poor eating habits will lead to health risks such as diabetes and heart disease eventually. Many of us get caught up in life so much so that we don't consider the Principle of Cause and Effect. The law states that nothing happens by chance, that chance is merely a term indicating cause existing but not recognized or perceived; that phenomena is continuous and without break or exception. So in other words, insufficient exercise and poor diets may lead to obesity, hypertension, diabetes, and even cancer. In most cases, obesity is the direct result of poor eating habits and is the root cause of many degenerative and often terminal diseases, not just the ones I previously mentioned. Cooking at home will cut back on your fast food habits. Cutting back on your fast food habits won't cure your obesity problem by itself, but it's a great place to begin. Less snack machine visits and more activity increases your metabolism, makes you feel good, and is a great start to creating healthy lifelong habits.

Cancer, high blood pressure, heart disease, and obesity, just to name a few, are all caused by poor healthy life choices. I know you hear of something else every week that causes cancer. It doesn't mean you have to put yourself in harms way by becoming a candidate for cancer. You can help yourself by preventing all forms of diseases as if your life depended on it and all you have to do is choose to eat right. Because choosing to eat right means choosing to live.

Gastrointestinal problems, lack of energy, and chronic nutritional deficiencies are other clues that you are not getting what you need from the snack machines, the quick-serve restaurants, or the fast food chains on your way to or from work. There is no need to wait until you have illnesses to look out for your own health. To be proactive means taking responsibility for your own well-being. It eventually costs less to spend the extra investment on good quality food than it does eating junk food. Everyone knows where the road to poor nutrition leads. Either Americans are playing ignorant or they have their priorities in the wrong place. Your entire life truly depends on what you eat. Let's take a closer look at this chain of events and hopefully you'll get a clearer picture:

> Jane is happily married to Bob.

> Jane and Bob have two young kids. Sue is four and Jan is five.

Jane was a stay-at-home mom for five years. She kept a happy and healthy home.

Jane enters the workforce and tries to prove to her boss that she is qualified for the position by working overtime.

Jane is juggling the responsibilities of motherhood and her career. Her career seems to be doing well.

Every morning, Jane prepares the kids for daycare, packs their lunch, and runs out the door.

On her way to work, Jane stops by Starbucks for her cappuccino and almond biscotti.

She skips lunch and instead snacks all day. Diet sodas and vending machine snacks seems to keep her energy levels up.

Jane rushes to pick up her children from daycare and prepares dinner.

Jane is mentally exhausted and famished.

Jane finally eats dinner with her family and has seconds.

Jane finds herself ordering carry out more often to save time.

Jane is tired yet unable to sleep, so she snacks on her favorite ice cream to calm and comfort her as she reviews the day's stressors in her mind.

Jane falls asleep in front of the television and finally retires at 11:30 pm.

Jane has no sex drive and her husband is frustrated.

Jane notices the pounds creeping up.

Jane visits her primary care provider, who in turn diagnoses her with hypothyroidism, hypertension, and high cholesterol.

Jane notices her daughter has a knack for music and dancing but knows that the extra curricula activities will require more of her time. Jane's already too tired with her existing schedule. She decides not to enroll her daughter in a program that will develop these latent skills.

Jane's boss offers her a management position if she enrolls in a business management program, which will take her 6 months to complete and require an extra 5 hours per week of her time. Jane's household can benefit from the increase in income, so she accepts the offer despite how she feels.

Jane notices that her hair is thinning and she is starting to develop hot flashes at the age of 37.

Jane continues her regiment and pays no attention to the signs. Jane is now 65 pounds overweight.

Jane is invited to family and friend events and gatherings but never seems to make it. Her exhaustion is getting the best of her.

Jane's husband is spending more time at work and less time at home.

Jane's daughter is beginning to develop behavioral problems, and they seem to be quarrelling more often.

Jane is staying in bed longer on her days off.

Jane is one of many people who seem to find themselves caught up in this vicious cycle, knowing where the path will ultimately lead. Why has Jane chosen to ignore the writing on the wall? This is the question of all time. Many people know what they need to do but don't do what they instinctively know. New research revealed that most American consumers read food labels for nutritional information. Many, however, do not let that get in the way of what they're going to buy. According to a poll by AP-Ipsos, 44% of consumers will still buy a product after reading a label that tells them that the item is loaded with calories, fat, and sugar. What this may indicate is that most people choose food based on how it makes them feel, its taste, and texture rather than its nutritional impact on the body. Again thereby solidifying the fact that many people choose not to help themselves despite the harm these choices may cause, just like Jane.

Jane will either come to her senses and make the connection between her food choices and the effect it has on her relationship with her spouse, her extended family and friends, her children and most importantly her health or go into a state of depression leading to a host of other conditions. Without the vital nutrients she needs to sustain a healthy body, she will not have the energy to exercise. Exercise gives the body more energy; like compound interest, it really adds up. Nor will she be able to think clearly and learn to manage her time effectively so she can spend quality time with her loved ones. There is an intricate connection between what Jane puts in her mouth and the quality of life she will ultimately lead. Remember, as for the body, garbage in and garbage out. The body will only perform as good as the fuel it's provided, short and simple. Spending a little time in the kitchen to cultivate your culinary skills beats a trip to the emergency room.

Let's talk about the sickness business. That's right; sickness is a business that keeps your doctors, the pharmaceutical drug companies, and the fast food chains' wallets fat and happy. Unfortunately, the sickness business has a few drawbacks that affect its consumers. It causes you to miss days at work. So how can you afford to keep this lucrative business operable if you lose time on the job? Seriously, how many sick days can you prevent yourself from having? I mean real sick days.

Right now, heart disease is rapidly increasing in women than it is in men. Whether there are more stressors in modern society or anxieties from balancing home and work, our diets can make all the difference. Muster up the strength to do everything you can to change your eating habits. For this is the key to overall health and wellness. Of course, there are no guarantees that you'll live a long life, but you certainly have control over the quality of life you will lead.

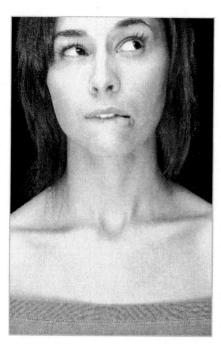

Like all fears and phobias, a cooking phobia is produced by the unconscious mind as a defensive mechanism. At some point in the past, there might have been an event involving cooking and emotional trauma, who knows. Maybe you had a dream you were being chased by a spatula with big gnawing teeth. Attaching emotions to circumstances is one of the primary ways that we as humans learn good and bad behaviors. Don't be afraid, you can wake up now. There are no utensils chasing you and you will not be attacked by a kitchen appliance as long as you follow the operational instructions.

Seriously, everyone has his or her own unique formula for when and how to feel bad. Food is a vehicle for nurturing people, a way of showing love, affection, and hospitality for breaking the ice socially, for expressing gratitude, for celebrating life, and so on. It also serves a myriad of emotional functions that have now become inseparably woven into the foundation of our interpersonal world. It's no wonder that many individuals become apprehensive about food preparation and cooking which leads to cooking phobia. If their meal falls short of expectation, there's a sense of failure, which may lead to a dread of not meeting needs and adversely affecting the emotional bond. Not to mention the feared anticipation of negative judgment, whether spoken or not.

Just remember, the more you learn and practice, the more confident you will become and ultimately triumph over your fear of cooking. Tony Robbins defines F.E.A.R. as an acronym for False Experience Appearing Real. So get out of your head, face your false experience, cultivate your skills through practice and self-education and you can overcome anything life has to offer.

So now will you reconsider your cooking phobia and face your F.E.A.R. head on? How can the kitchen—a place of sustenance, where warm feelings of motherly nurturance and sweet aromas reminiscent of childhood days gone by—be a place of trepidation? Cooking can in fact be a fun, humbling, ceremonious, and revitalizing experience that has the capacity to yield health and wellness for you and your loved ones for years to come. Try it, and you'll discover that it holds the enduring key to life!

CHAPTER 5

THE UNTAPPED POWER OF WOMEN IN THE KITCHEN

Throughout history, women have been seen as being caretakers and nurturers of the family. Some even believe that a woman's biology, including the fact that she gives birth, makes her uniquely suited for this role. Whatever the reason, the fact remains that even today, when women have become assertive enough to go outside the home and make a name and a career for themselves, in many cases, they continue to be the caregivers and nurturers in the home. The kitchen is where this care and nurturing takes concrete shape. When there is lack of support, women feel trapped by this role and they start resenting their time in the kitchen.

Yet cooking and the kitchen are far more than exercising the caring and nurturing role. For hundreds of years, most homes did not even have a room called a kitchen. Food was cooked next to either the table, or where people ate their meals, and all the members of the family shared the sights, sounds, and smells of cooking. If food and its preparation were of primary importance, the place where cooking happened was the center of the home. Everyone met there, shared there, laughed there, and ate there.

This cooking center evolved around the woman. For example, while most people think of males as the strong, big chiefs of Indian tribes, the women played an essential and integral role in Indian life. Women were extremely important in the farming and agriculture of their food, which represented a large part of Indian life. The food eaten was from the earth, none of it was wasted, and among all else, resourcefulness was well regarded.

Women carried on the tradition of what Margaret Rosler calls "accumulating and demonstrating cultural capital." She was the custodian of food culture and the culture of her people, she carried forth the heritage of food preparation, and she was the inventor of new ways of cooking and discoverer of new truths about food. In addition, as her power was truly enormous and all pervasive, she, along with her food, became relegated to the background. Cooking became a "chore" and the kitchen was created—an exclusive workplace where she could quickly finish the "chore" and then rejoin humankind: her family.

For many women, liberation meant rejecting the kitchen and all that went with it. Moreover, this rejection has meant a tremendous loss of cultural capital. America is a country of many people who came together from five continents and brought with them their many colorful cultures, mixed and merged to make new ones. However, in a few decades, this cultural genesis of over two centuries was destroyed. Take breakfast for example. The traditional American breakfast was huge business—waffles, homemade cereals, grits, numerous kinds of hot biscuits with gravy, salmon or cod hash, muffins, chops, and even soups, all besides the present eggs. It was full of calories of course, but it was a culture of tolerance, innovation, and of pioneering spirit. And what do we have instead of this today? A meager juice, coffee, and toast. And of course, the much touted "choice"—a choice between which brand of cereals to eat (and whether it should be salted, sweet, fortified with iron and vitamins, or coated with chocolate), which brand of bread, and which brand of juice. Forcing us further down the path of branded choices is the new image of woman—definitely not one who "slaves" in the kitchen, but the thin woman, the anorexic woman. This woman who is beaming at us day in and day out until we feel so guilty at even thinking about food that the kitchen is the last place we want to be.

We need to take back control over how we are portrayed by the media. We need to exercise true choice, rather than the limited corporate choices offered to us. What better way than to take control of what we choose to eat. To revel in the power we have at our fingertips to choose what we want to eat, how we want to eat it, and what effect we want it to have on our bodies and our minds. To be able to say NO to mindless uniformity of pizzas and hotdogs and burgers and French fries that add unhealthy weight and turn us into anorexics or bulimics. To say YES to diversity, to freshness, to experimentation, to history, and finally to culture. Amen!

This power can be ours today, without having to renounce any other aspects of our lives. The wealth of kitchen appliances that are available make cooking what and how we want a wave of the magic wand rather than a chore. The Crock-Pot replaces the dying embers of a hearth, where food was cooked slowly. The mincers, slicers, mixers, and juicers take away the tediousness and drudgery of preparation of food. Ovens offer us an enormous choice of ways to make food enticing. In addition, the refrigerator and deep freezer puts all ingredients at our fingertips and brings us back to the fundamentals of wholesome living that our ancestors have worked so hard to preserve—giving us a taste of our cultural roots which fuels our mind, body, and our spirits.

The power of the woman in the kitchen is very visible today. Witness the migration to the kitchen that typically occur at most social gatherings. The kitchen has always been and will always be the hub of caring and nurturing, of interaction, of innovation, of expressing creativity. Man or woman, the kitchen is and will always remain the place of true power.

CHAPTER 6

THE MODERN LIFESTYLE AND FOOD

Modern America: the land of beauty, wealth, and innovative technology. Technology has helped us streamline our lives, giving us the opportunity to pursue careers, expand our knowledge, and learn new tools, trades, languages, and even instruments. We can text-message our spouses, listen to our favorite music on an I-pod, and use a laptop to research a stock tip all at the same time.

Despite the wealth of information, technological tools, gadgets, and gizmos that are created for our convenience, Americans are still developing chronic and degenerative conditions. We contract cancers, diabetes, cardiovascular disorders, and obesity at alarming rates. Every day, more and more of us are dying slow and vicious deaths with an eating utensil: the unassuming fork.

With all the conveniences of technology, we have no time to step into the kitchen and cook ourselves a healthy meal to ensure that we continue to enjoy these amazing times. Our diet and lifestyle controls our concentration, energy levels, and mood swings. Bad nutrition and diet habits have been blamed for the increase in diagnoses of ADD, ADHD, and other attention-deficit disorders.

Our busy lives influence what we eat. If we are too busy to cook, we may or may not develop ADD or bipolar disorders, but we stand a better chance of living with increased stress, irritability, and depression. Yes, it's obvious that the daily grinds of life can often influence the things you eat and may even satisfy your immediate needs. But in the long term, you will inevitably feel the effects of your ill choices.

Grabbing something quick may be convenient for now, but what it does to your body is everlasting. Modern food processing has altered the types of fatty acids we consume. Everything is created to be able to sit on the shelves for long periods at a time. It needs to sit there as long as it takes you to be enticed by the advertisements to buy it. It's no surprise that all the experts speak about the "dumbing down" of America. Our brains are mostly composed of fatty acids. We are not feeding our brains. That's why we're irritable and can't concentrate.

Now, more than ever, we are more prone to consume man-made chemicals. For example, food coloring and other products we consume are made with petroleum. Maybe, we can save money, if instead of putting the gas pump in our gas lines we put it up to our lips to drink. Snack foods high in sugar, Trans fats, and carbohydrates consume more aisles in the grocery stores than anything else does. Yes, they are convenient for a quick energy boost that dies hard and fast, but they deteriorate the quality of your temple (your body). Those sugars and carbohydrates increase your insulin levels. Your body stores food just eaten as fat when your insulin level is high. Therefore, your brain is deprived of food because it's only burning sugar.

It's estimated that one-third of U.S. adults are obese. The Centers for Disease Control and Prevention defines obesity as an excessively high amount of body fat or adipose tissue in relation to lean body mass. The amount of body fat (or adiposity) includes concern for both the distribution of fat throughout the body and the size of the adipose tissue deposits. Body fat distribution can be estimated by skin-fold measures, waist-to-hip circumference ratios, or techniques such as ultrasound, computed tomography, or magnetic resonance imaging. BMI or Basal Metabolic Rate is a common measure expressing the relationship (or ratio) of weight-to-height. It is a mathematical formula in which a person's body weight in kilograms is divided by the square of his or her height in meters (i.e., wt/(ht)2. The BMI is more highly correlated with body fat than any other indicator of height and weight. Individuals with a BMI of 25 to 29.9 are considered overweight, while individuals with a BMI of 30 or more are considered obese. The percentage of children and adolescents who are defined as obese has more than doubled since the early 1970s. Obesity has a lasting effect on us. Your children may suffer the cruelty of other children teasing them at school or in gym class. If they are taunted when they try to become active, it will deter them from getting involved in future activities. There is nothing more lasting than death, and obesity may cause pre-mature death. In this stage in life, what you do or not do in your kitchen affects your families lives as well as your own.

The average meal in this country is getting larger. If you cook your meals at home, you have more control of what and how much you eat. If you go to fast food restaurants and they give you larger portions, you will eat it more. Exercise self-control. Decide that you don't want to be super-sized and choose to have a healthy, smaller meal cooked in your own home. Just because there is a bargain buffet doesn't mean you have to make sure you get more than your money's worth to stick it back to the man. You are not hurting the restaurant. They are already overcharging you and providing you with inferior products. They have already made their money off you. You are hurting yourself by overeating.

The rate at which we eat has changed as well. We are too busy to take our time and savor our foods. It takes about 15-20 minutes before our stomach will get the message to our brain that we are full. If we are finished with the entire meal in ten minutes, most likely we are going to go back for seconds on dessert before we realize we are full.

Chewing your food slowly and enjoying the different flavors, textures, and aromas can evoke a sense of contentment and being in the present moment. You will be able to extract most of the nutrients from the food you are eating because you are taking your time to chew. Digestion begins in the mouth through the masticating process of the molars. When you chew slowly, you are ensuring that your body is receiving as much nutrients as the food you are ingesting can provide. Not to mention the fact that by the time you complete the meal you attended with such mind-full awareness, you'll be too full for seconds. Keep this up and in about a month, who knows, you just might be 1 to 2 sizes smaller!

We can easily change our lifestyle. Lifestyle changes can help you decrease stress. There is enough stress being a part of a community, having a job, and raising children. You can make things easier on yourself if your body feels good. Now, studies are showing eating disorders are not only popular among teens, but a growing number of adults are now showing signs of eating disorders. There is a lot of pressure from our fast-paced world to look a certain way, but some of this also comes from the lack of information given to the average consumer.

It's time for America to wake up from this bewildered state and start making educated decisions about their health and the food they consume. Corporate America, God bless them, is only responding to your lack of desire to self-educate. Without self-direction, you become the benefactor of exploitative capitalism. The effects of the media's influence on children has been well documented, which is why the average 12-year-old can talk their parents into putting that sugar-laden box of Cocoa Puffs into their shopping cart.

CHAPTER 7

RE-DISCOVERING WHOLESOME AND NATURAL FOOD

Mostly, the entire model of food has changed: adapted to meet the ever-demanding needs of hectic America. Unless you grow all of your food in your own garden and prepare all of your meals from scratch, it's virtually impossible to eat food without preservatives added by manufacturers during processing. Most manufacturers add preservatives primarily to help prevent spoilage during the time it takes to transport foods over long distances to stores and ultimately to our kitchens.

Before you can fully understand whole foods, you need to know more about the nemesis of real food: man-made chemicals. As the adage goes, wherever there is smoke, there is fire. Similarly, wherever there is fast, adulterated food, there is the possibility for disease. Preservatives, however, can be both friend and foe. There are natural methods for extending the shelf life of food without having to purchase foods that are laden with man-made chemicals. This topic will be discussed in subsequent chapters.

There are over 12,000 man-made chemicals added to our American food supply today, and that number continues to rise. Food additives are not natural nutrition for humans or pets. Today, millions of Americans are suffering with allergies that in many cases are the result of food additives because of long-term exposure to these food chemicals from infancy. The human body was not designed to be exposed to that degree of chemicals and food additives, and it's only a matter of time before the immune system begins to break down or becomes over-reactive.

By and large, people are unaware of the types of chemicals and food additives they are consuming and the long-term side effects they create. Let's begin by understanding what food additives are and their purpose. What is a food additive? In its broadest sense, a food additive is any substance added to food. From the FDA's legal perspective, it means "any substance with an intended use which results or may reasonably be expected to result—directly or indirectly—in its becoming a component or otherwise affecting the characteristics of any food." This description comprises of any substance used in the production, processing, treatment, packaging, transportation, or storage of food.

Additives are used in foods for five main reasons:

- To maintain product consistency, for example, emulsifiers give products a consistent texture and prevent them from separating.

- To improve or maintain nutritional value. Vitamins and minerals are added to many common foods such as milk, flour, cereal, and margarine to make up for those likely to be lacking in a person's diet or lost in processing. Such fortification and enrichment has helped reduce malnutrition among the U.S. population.

- To maintain palatability and wholesomeness. Preservatives retard product spoilage caused by mold, air, bacteria, fungi, or yeast. Bacterial contamination can cause food-borne illness, including life-threatening botulism. Antioxidants are preservatives that prevent fats and oils in baked goods and other foods from becoming rancid or developing an off-flavor. They also prevent cut-fresh fruits such as apples from turning brown when exposed to air.

- To provide leavening or control acidity/alkalinity. Leavening agents that release acids when heated can react with baking soda to help cakes, biscuits, and other baked goods to rise during baking. Other additives help modify the acidity and alkalinity of foods for proper flavor, taste, and color.

- To enhance flavor or impart desired color. Many spices and natural and synthetic flavors enhance the taste of foods. Colors, likewise, enhance the appearance of certain foods to meet consumer expectations.

Although there are several good benefits for using additives, there are a myriad of food chemicals and additives that many people ought to avoid. Here are the top ten:

Acesulfame K
Known commercially as Sunette or Sweet One, acesulfame is a sugar substitute sold in packet or tablet form, in chewing gum, dry mixes for beverages, instant coffee and tea, gelatin desserts, puddings, and non-dairy creamers. Tests show that the additive cause's cancer in animals, which means it, may increase cancer in humans. Avoid acesulfame K and products containing it. Your sweet tooth isn't worth it.

Artificial colorings
The great bulk of artificial colorings used in food are synthetic dyes. For decades, synthetic food dyes have been suspected of being toxic or carcinogenic and many have been banned. Whenever possible, choose foods without dyes. They're mostly used in foods of questionable nutritional worth anyway. Natural ingredients should provide all the color your food needs.

Aspartame
This sugar substitute, sold commercially as Equal and NutraSweet, was hailed

as the savior for dieters who for decades had put up with saccharin's unpleasant aftertaste. There are quite a few problems with aspartame. The first is phenylketonuria (PKU). One out of 20,000 babies is born without the ability to metabolize phenylalanine, one of the two amino acids in aspartame. Toxic levels of this substance in the blood can result in mental retardation. Beyond PKU, several scientists believe that aspartame might cause altered brain function and behavior changes in consumers. And many people (though a minuscule fraction) have reported dizziness, headaches, epileptic-like seizures, and menstrual problems after ingesting aspartame.

Avoid aspartame if you are pregnant, suffer from PKU, or think that you experience side effects from using it. If you consume more than a couple of servings a day, consider cutting back. And, to be on the safe side, don't give aspartame to infants.

BHA & BHT
These two closely related chemicals are added to oil-containing foods to prevent oxidation and retard rancidity. The International Agency for Research on Cancer, part of the World Health Organization, considers BHA to be possibly carcinogenic to humans, and the State of California has listed it as a carcinogen. Some studies show the same cancer-causing possibilities for BHT. BHT and BHA are totally unnecessary. To avoid them, read the label. Because of the possibility that BHT and BHA might cause cancer, both should be eliminated from our food supply.

Caffeine
Caffeine is found naturally in tea, coffee, and cocoa. It is also added to many soft drinks. It is one of the few drugs—a stimulant—added to foods. Caffeine promotes stomach-acid secretion (possibly increasing the symptoms of peptic ulcers), temporarily raises blood pressure, and dilates some blood vessels while constricting others. Excessive caffeine intake results in "caffeinism," with symptoms ranging from nervousness to insomnia. These problems also affect children who drink between 2 to 7 cans of soda a day. Caffeine may also interfere with reproduction and affect developing fetuses. Experiments on lab animals link caffeine to birth defects such as cleft palates, missing fingers and toes, and skull malformations.

Caffeine is mildly addictive, which is why some people experience headaches when they stop drinking it. While small amounts of caffeine don't pose a problem for everyone, avoid it if you are trying to become or are pregnant. And try to keep caffeine out of you child's diet.
Note: Caffeine can be ingested in cases of severe migraine headaches to quickly relieve pain due to its dilating effects.

Monosodium glutamate (MSG)

A Japanese chemist identified MSG as the substance in certain seasonings that added to the flavor of protein-containing foods. Unfortunately, too much MSG can lead to headaches, tightness in the chest, and a burning sensation in the forearms and the back of the neck. If you think you are sensitive to MSG, look at ingredient listings. Also, avoid hydrolyzed vegetable protein, or HVP, which may contain MSG.

Nitrite and nitrate

Sodium nitrite and sodium nitrate are two closely related chemicals used for centuries to preserve meat. While nitrate itself is harmless, it is readily converted to nitrite. When nitrite combines with compounds called secondary amines, it forms nitrosamines, extremely powerful cancer-causing chemicals. The chemical reaction occurs most readily at the high temperatures of frying. Nitrite has long been suspected as being a cause of stomach cancer. Look for nitrite-free processed meats, some of which are frozen (refrigeration reduces the need for nitrites), at some health food and grocery stores. However, regardless of the presence of nitrite or nitrosamines, the high fat, high-sodium content of most processed meats should be enough to discourage you from choosing them. And don't cook with bacon drippings.

Olestra

Olestra, the fake fat recently approved by the Food and Drug Administration (FDA), is both dangerous and unnecessary. Olestra was approved over the objection of dozens of leading scientists.

The additive may be fat-free but it has a fatal side effect: it attaches to valuable nutrients and flushes them out of the body. Some of these nutrients, called carotenoids, appear to protect us from such diseases as lung cancer, prostate cancer, heart disease, and macular degeneration. The Harvard School of Public Health states that "the long-term consumption of olestra snack foods might therefore result in several thousand unnecessary deaths each year from lung and prostate cancers and heart disease and hundreds of additional cases of blindness in the elderly due to macular degeneration. Besides contributing to disease, olestra causes diarrhea and other serious gastrointestinal problems, even at low doses."

The FDA certified olestra despite the fact that there are safe low-fat snacks already on the market. There is no evidence to show that olestra will have any significant effect on reducing obesity in America.

Despite being approved as safe by the FDA, all snacks containing olestra must carry a warning label (similar to one found on cigarettes) that states:

This product contains olestra. Olestra may cause abdominal cramping and loose stools. Olestra inhibits the absorption of some vitamins and other nutrients. Vitamins A, D, E, and K have been added.

CSPI advises consumers to avoid all olestra foods and urges major food manufacturers not to make olestra-containing products.

Potassium bromate
This additive has long been used to increase the volume of bread and to produce bread with a fine crumb (the non-crust part of bread) structure. Most bromate rapidly breaks down to form innocuous bromide. However, bromate itself causes cancer in animals. The tiny amounts of bromate that may remain in bread pose a small risk to consumers. Bromate has been banned virtually worldwide except in Japan and the United States. It is rarely used in California because a cancer warning is required on the label.

Sulfites
Sulfites are a class of chemicals that can keep cut fruits and vegetables looking fresh. They also prevent discoloration in apricots, raisins, and other dried fruits; control "black spot" in freshly caught shrimp; and prevent discoloration, bacterial growth, and fermentation in wine. Until the early 1980s they were considered safe, but CSPI found six scientific studies proving that sulfites could provoke sometimes-severe allergic reactions. CSPI and the Food and Drug Administration (FDA) identified at least a dozen fatalities linked to sulfites. All of the deaths occurred among asthmatics. In 1985, Congress finally forced the FDA to ban sulfites from most fruits and vegetables. Especially if you have asthma, be sure to consider whether your attacks might be related to sulfites. The ban does not cover fresh-cut potatoes, dried fruits, and wine.

Now that you've been enlightened on the subject of food additives, you are now ready to re-discover the power of whole foods and the health benefits that ensue. Whole foods by definition are foods that are as close to their natural state as possible. For example, an orange is a whole food, as opposed to commercially prepared orange juice, or a bowl of brown rice as opposed to Uncle Ben's ten-minute white rice. Whole foods have had little to no processing and retain most, if not all, of their original nutrients and fiber. A benefit of eating whole foods is that they retain their natural flavor and so, once we've had a taste of the real thing, we notice the full, naturally sweet and rich flavor of many vegetables, grains, nuts, and fruits.

Whole foods are foods that are unprocessed or processed as little as possible. Often they are confused with organic foods. Simply put, they are foods in their whole state. Examples of whole foods include unpolished grain, both conventional and organically grown fruits and vegetables. Most grains are "polished," meaning that they take away the grains outer coating that contains selenium an important antioxidant mineral. The processing is done for longer shelf life and to enable faster cooking. Try to avoid quick-cooking products such as instant oatmeal, as these are heavily processed. Another non-whole food product is fruit juice because it lacks fiber, so when you drink fruit juice you are drinking sugar water with some vitamins and minerals. Eat whole fruit; its fiber slows down the digestion of the fruit's sugar content.

The following list is but an example of health benefits you can gain from whole foods:

Apples lower cholesterol and risk for cancer and have mild antibacterial, antiviral, anti-inflammatory estrogenic activity. High in fiber, apples help avoid constipation and suppress appetite.

Asparagus is an excellent source of the antioxidant glutathione that helps lower the risk of cancer.

Avocado benefits blood circulation, lowers cholesterol, and helps dilate blood vessels. Its main fat, monounsaturated oleic acid, acts as an antioxidant to block artery-destroying toxicity caused by cholesterol.

Banana and plantain help sooth the stomach. Good for upset stomach, they strengthen the stomach lining against acid and ulcers.

Barley reduces cholesterol and has anti-viral and anti-cancer activity. It also contains powerful antioxidants, including tocotrienols.

Beans are a potent medicine that helps lower cholesterol. It also regulates blood sugar levels, making it an excellent food for diabetics.

Beets are richer than spinach in iron and other minerals. The greens are helpful in cases of anemia, tuberculosis, constipation, poor appetite, obesity, tumors, gout, pimples, and so on. Beets are one of the best foods to relieve constipation and are good for obesity.

Bell peppers are rich in antioxidant Vitamin C, thereby helps fight colds, asthma, bronchitis, respiratory infections, cataracts, macular degeneration, and cancer.

Blueberries act as a strange type of antibiotic by blocking the attachment of bacteria that cause urinary tract infections. They also contain chemicals that curb diarrhea.

Broccoli is a unique package of versatile disease-fighters as it is abundant in antioxidants, including quercetin, glutathione, beta-carotene, indoles, Vitamin C, and so on. Broccoli is extremely high in cancer-fighting activity, particularly effective against lung, colon, and breast cancers. It speeds up the removal of estrogen from the body, helping suppress breast cancer. It is also a super source of chromium, which helps control insulin and blood sugar.

Brussels sprouts possess some of the same powers as broccoli and cabbage. Brussels sprouts are excellent for anti-cancer, estrogenic, and packed with various antioxidants and indoles.

Cabbage contains numerous anti-cancer and antioxidant compounds, speeds up estrogen metabolism, and is thought to help block breast cancer and a prelude to colon cancer.

Carrot is an excellent source of beta-carotene, a powerful anti-cancer, artery-protecting, immune-boosting, infection-fighting antioxidant with wide protective powers. The high soluble fiber in carrots reduces blood cholesterol and encourages regularity. Cooking carrots before consumption can make it easier for the body to absorb carrot's beta-carotene.

Cauliflower contains many of the same cancer-fighting, hormone-regulating compounds as broccoli and cabbage.

Celery is a natural cure for high blood pressure. Celery also contains eight different families of anti-cancer compounds, such as phthalates and polyacetylenes that detoxify carcinogens, especially cigarette smoke.

As is clearly visible from the above examples, whole foods are excellent for our health and should be made a part of our daily diet.

TOTAL NUTRITION KITCHEN MAKEOVER™

Are you running low on energy? Check out how much energy you can jump-start your day with nature's fast food and it's even fat-free:

Description	Quantity	Energy (calories)	Carbs (gms)	Protein (gms)	Weight (gms)	Fat (gms)	Sat. fat (gms)
Orange juice	1 cup	105	25	1	249	0	0
Orange raw	1 cup	110	26	2	248	0	0.1
Apple sauce canned sweetened	1 cup	195	51	0	255	0	0.1
Apple sauce unsweetened-d	1 cup	105	28	0	244	0	0
Blueberries sweetened	10 oz	230	62	1	284	0	0
Blueberries raw	1 cup	80	20	1	145	1	0
Peaches canned	1 cup	190	51	1	256	0	0
Peaches raw	1 cup	75	19	1	170	0	0
Pineapple canned	1 cup	200	52	1	255	0	0
Pineapple raw	1 cup	75	19	1	155	0	0
Plums canned	1 cup	230	60	1	258	0	0
Plums raw	1 plum	15	4	0	28	0	0

CHAPTER 8

HOW TO GET MOST OF YOUR NUTRITION FROM THESE SUPER FOODS

Certain foods that you buy from the stores have a higher nutritional value than others. Most of them have some sort of an effect on the body, ranging from positive to negative. That is why we eat food, for the nutrition and energy it gives us to keep on living and performing our daily chores. There are things that you can do to get the most from your nutritional experiences. The following super foods—as opposed to vitamins or supplements—are foods that naturally concentrate important nutrients. Unlike dietary supplements or vitamins taken in isolation, super foods provide many nutrients that support each other and prevent the kind of imbalances that inevitably occurs when vitamins are taken in single form.

Do we really need these so-called super foods? In theory, if the food you eat is whole, rich, complete, and varied, we should need nothing more to supplement our daily diet; but can even the most meticulous and health conscientious among us say that our diet is or has been perfect all the time? With the depletion of our soils, the widespread use of additives, and the prevalence of sugar, refined carbohydrates and rancid vegetable oils, which all of us have invariably ingested—if not in adulthood, at least in our youth—no one living in an industrialized society today can say that his/her diet has been perfect. For those unwilling or unable to give up bad habits like caffeine, alcohol, or smoking, a daily supply of super foods is necessary.

The following short list is not meant to be a comprehensive compendium of super foods, but only a few examples of these fortifying foods ingested on a daily basis can make a major difference in your health and well-being and can, in general, be taken by everyone.

***Keep in mind that certain herbal products used for specific ailments are best taken with the advice of a holistic health practitioner for proper dosage recommendation.

Fulvic Mineral: Fulvic, a natural ionic molecule, is rapidly being recognized as an important key in many scientific breakthroughs of the 21st century. Fulvic is one of the most crucial factors in the reversal and prevention of disease, as well as the maintenance of good health. Nature made it abundantly obtainable, but like many things, man has interfered with this vital process and it is no longer available in adequate quantities in the foods we eat.
Fulvic is created by microbial activity at the roots of plants. Its function is to dissolve and convert the metallic- and clay-based mineral molecules that are in soils into a form that is usable by plants, animals, and people. Once the minerals are dissolved, plants uptake, through their root system, the powerful Fulvic substance that is loaded with dissolved minerals and trace elements.

Fulvic is an immense arsenal of powerful phytochemicals, biochemicals, supercharged antioxidants, free-radical scavengers, nutrients, enzymes, hormones, amino acids, antibiotics, antivirals, and antifungals. Without Fulvic, many of the vital chemical reactions required by the body to make use of nutrients are impossible. For example, vitamins cannot be absorbed by the body unless minerals are present.

ORAC Super Fruit Powder: Extraordinary scientific research from Tufts University has evaluated the antioxidant needs of the average person PLUS the antioxidant power (referred to as Oxygen Radical Absorbance Capacity or ORAC Value) of fruits and vegetables. Their research has concluded that we need approximately 5,000 ORAC units per day to have a significant impact on plasma and tissue antioxidant capacity. Consumption of a minimum of three servings of fruits and vegetables per day provides approximately 1200 ORAC units. This means the average person is short by approximately 3,800 ORAC units each day, depending on the fruits and vegetables they are choosing.
ORAC+ fills the gap to "mop-up" all the body's free radical generation on a daily basis to slow the aging process (anti-aging). ORAC+ has been independently tested by one of the world's foremost laboratories specializing in Oxygen Radical Absorbing Capacity (ORAC). Oxygen Radical Absorbance Capacity (ORAC) measures the total "antioxidant power" of foods and nutrients by calculating the ability of a product to protect against potentially damaging oxygen-free radicals.
Free radicals are molecules that harm healthy body cells. The accumulated damage caused by free radicals is considered a primary cause of the aging process. You can dramatically slow down this aging process by combating free radical activity with antioxidants.

Acerola Tablets: A berry rich in ascorbic acid, acerola provides Vitamin C with numerous cofactors, including bioflavonoids and rutin, to optimize the body's uptake and use of ascorbic acid. Vitamin C, the most important dietary antioxidant, was popularized by Linus Pauling, who recommends taking pure ascorbic acid in amounts up to 15 grams a day for a variety of ailments. However, large quantities of Vitamin C may be harmful to the kidneys and can lead to deficiencies in bioflavonoids. Only small quantities of natural Vitamin C in the form of acerola tablets can provide the same protection as large amounts of pure ascorbic acid without the side effects.

Bee Pollen: Famous athletes who take bee pollen regularly for strength and endurance have popularized it. It has been used successfully to treat a variety of ailments, including allergies, asthma, menstrual irregularities, constipation, diarrhea, anemia, low energy, cancer, rheumatism, arthritis, and toxic conditions. A Russian study of the inhabitants of the province of Georgia, where many live to 100 years and a few to age 150, revealed that many of these centenarians were beekeepers who often ate raw, unprocessed honey with all its "impurities," that is, with the pollen. Bee pollen contains 22 amino acids including the eight essential ones, 27 minerals and the full gamut of vitamins, hormones, and fatty acids. Most importantly, bee pollen contains more than 5,000 enzymes and coenzymes. It is the presence of enzymes, many of which have immediate detoxifying effects, that sometimes provokes allergic reactions in those taking bee pollen for the first time. If this happens, start with very small amounts and slowly build up to a tablespoon or so per day. Some brands are more easily tolerated than others. Avoid pollen that has been dried at temperatures higher than 130°. Bee pollen can be taken in powder, capsule, or tablet form—or in raw unprocessed honey mixed with cereal or spread on toast.

Blue-Green Algae, Spirulina and Chlorella: Blue-green micro algae, and its cousins spirulina and chlorella, grow on inland waters throughout the world—visible as greenish scum on still lakes and ponds. The Aztecs ate it as a staple food, dried and spread on tortillas. Africans of the Sahara region also use dried spirulina with grains and vegetables. These algae are high in protein, carotenoids, and minerals. Beware, however, of claims that they can provide Vitamin B12 in vegetarian diets. Nevertheless, the high mineral and protein content of the various algae make them an excellent super food, a good supplement to the diet, and a useful product for the treatment of a variety of health problems. Of the three main types of algae, spirulina is said to be the easiest to digest and absorb, because its cell walls are composed of mucopolysaccharides rather than indigestible cellulose. Chlorella needs special processing to improve digestibility of a tough outer cell wall, but it is valued for its ability to bind with heavy metals and carry them out of the body. Wild blue-green algae is said to have remarkable healing properties but can transform into an exceptionally toxic plant under certain conditions. Freeze-drying is said to denature these toxins.

Bitters: Herbal extracts of bitter, mineral-rich herbs are a traditional tonic for stimulating the bile and increasing digestion and assimilation of fats. They often are the best remedy for calming a queasy stomach. Floradix makes one such product. Another is Swedish Bitters, originally formulated by Paracelsus and later "rediscovered" by a Swedish scientist. Bitters supply nutrients from bitter leaves that are often lacking in the Western diet. Many cultures, including the Chinese and Hindu, value bitter herbs for their cleansing, strengthening, and healing properties.

High Vitamin Butter: Deep yellow butter oil from cows eating rapidly growing green grass supplies not only vitamins A and D but also the X Factor, discovered by Dr. Weston Price. It can be used as a supplement to regular dietary butter, particularly during winter and early spring.

Cod Liver Oil: Once a standard supplement in traditional European societies, cod liver oil provides fat-soluble vitamins A and D, which Dr. Price found present in the diet of primitives in amounts ten times higher than the typical American diet of his day. Cod liver oil supplements are necessary for women and their male partners, to be taken for several months before conception, and for women during pregnancy. Growing children will also benefit greatly from a small daily dose. Cod liver oil is also rich in eicosapentaenoic acid (EPA). The body makes this fatty acid from omega-3 linolenic acid as an important link in the chain of fatty acids that ultimately results in prostaglandins, localized tissue hormones. It is very important for the proper function of the brain and nervous system. Those individuals who have consumed large amounts of polyunsaturated oils, especially hydrogenated oils, or who have impaired pancreatic function, such as diabetics, may not be able to produce EPA and will, therefore, lack important prostaglandins unless they consume oily fish or take a cod liver oil supplement. Buy cod liver oil in dark bottles and store in a cool, dark, dry place. Some studies indicate that cod liver oil is toxic in large amounts, so don't overdo it (1 teaspoon per day is a good rule for adults, half that for children). It's easy to take when stirred into a small amount of water. Dr. Price always gave cod liver oil with butter oil, extracted by centrifuge from good quality spring or fall butter. He found that cod liver oil on its own was relatively ineffective, but combined with butter oil produced excellent results. Your diet should include both good quality, organic butter and cod liver oil.

Evening Primrose Oil, Borage Oil or Black Currant Oil: These oils contain a fatty acid called gamma-linolenic acid, or GLA, which the body produces from omega-6 linoleic acid by the action of special enzymes. In many individuals, the production or effectiveness of this enzyme is compromised, especially as they grow older. Malnutrition, consumption of hydrogenated oils, and diabetes inhibit the conversion of omega-6 linoleic acid to GLA. GLA-rich oils have been used to treat cancer, premenstrual syndrome, breast disease, scleroderma, colitis, irritable bowel syndrome, and cystic fibrosis. They have been shown to increase liver function and mental acuity.

Kelp: Like all sea vegetables, kelp provides minerals found in seawater, especially iodine and trace minerals that may be lacking in our depleted soils. For Westerners unaccustomed to including seaweeds in the diet, a small daily supplement of kelp in tablet or powdered form is a good idea, but don't overdo it—excess iodine may also cause thyroid problems.

Noni Juice: Juice of the Tahitian noni fruit is revered by the Polynesians for its curative powers, possibly due to the presence of an alkaloid precursor called xeronine, which contributes to the effectiveness of proteins on the cellular level. Noni juice has been used successfully to treat blood sugar problems, injuries and pain, digestive disorders, depression, and many other ailments. It should be taken on an empty stomach.

Wheat Germ Oil: Expeller-expressed wheat germ oil is an excellent source of natural Vitamin E, which is our best natural protection for the cell membrane. The Shute brothers of Canada demonstrated that Vitamin E supplements are an effective protection against heart disease. In their studies, they used wheat germ oil, not synthetic Vitamin E preparations.

Yeast: Dried nutritional yeast is an excellent natural source of B complex vitamins (except for B12) plus a variety of minerals. Look for yeast that has been processed at low temperatures. Yeast does not contribute to Candida as has been claimed—Candida feeds on refined carbohydrates not yeast. The late eminent physician Dr. Henry Bieler treated many cases of chronic fatigue with yeast supplements.

Glyconutrients: Scientists today have recently discovered that these vital nutrients are greatly missing in our diet. After years of research, many have come to the conclusion that the lack of these specific sugars is a major reason for most of today's diseases. What are glyconutrients?

Glyconutrients are nutrients, or in technical terms, a monosaccharide, that we don't get in today's diet because we no longer forage for our food off the land and, as a result we don't access these sugars that can be found in plant roots and fungus, for example. A glyconutrient complex is a proprietary blend of plant-derived sugars that is needed by the cells of your body. They are mannose, galactose, fucose, xylose, glucose, N-Acetylglucosamine, N-acetylneuraminic acid, and N-acetylgalactosamine. Complete glyconutrition provides immune stability, strengthening, and maintenance. There are over 20,000 studies conducted annually on glycoforms alone. Researchers from universities and major pharmaceutical companies recognize the importance of this new discovery. Breaking the "sugar-code" will mean a tremendous advancement in health and medicine.

Now that you have stocked your cabinets and refrigerator with these fortifying super foods, let's address the whole foods for your meals. Let's start with the shopping. You're going to need to start purchasing more fruits, vegetables, and the right carbohydrates we talked about earlier. Consider buying organically grown produce as opposed to commercially or conventionally grown as they have less pesticides, insecticides, and growth hormones, and they are not genetically modified. For your meats and seafood, buy from reputable sources. Try to always buy fresh deep ocean seafood, as they have less contaminants and heavy metals than their farm-raised counterparts. Don't be afraid to ask the butcher where your fish was caught. Pre-packaged seafood may have added preservatives that you really don't want or need in your body. For those of you who aren't vegetarians (which is a large part of the western society), choose your meat wisely and with trepidation. Most meat today is poisonous. If not organically raised, more than likely you are consuming meat or chicken that has been injected with growth hormones, antibiotics, preserved with BHT, and irradiated.

The next step is to clean your kitchen thoroughly. Use environmentally friendly products to keep your kitchen free of parasites and harmful bacteria. Studies have shown that our kitchens contain more dangerous bacteria than our bathrooms. Therefore, if you are not in the mood to bite down on your toilet seat, keep the kitchen free of bacteria.

Observe safe food handling guidelines. Some of the meats we buy have handling instruction stickers on them. Read the stickers. Follow the handling instructions to reduce exposure to bacteria to yourself and your family. If one of you is contaminated, there is a good chance that the viruses caused may be passed around to everyone in the house. Therefore wash your foods thoroughly. If you have not made the right decision to go organic, then your fruits and vegetables will be contaminated with pesticides. Don't place washed produce back into the same containers they came in. Make sure you wash away the pesticides thoroughly before eating vegetables, fruits, or other products. Fish and seafood should be cleaned, gutted, and washed as soon as you get home before re-wrapped tightly in new containers and frozen. Clean your meats thoroughly as well before cooking.

Clean your hands, utensils, and food surfaces. Yes, you already cleaned the kitchen before you started cooking, but it can't hurt to make sure you are extra careful. Clean countertops after they have been exposed to raw meats and foods. Wash dishcloths often and preferably in the hot cycle. Dishcloths carry many billions of bacteria and require constant cleaning. Keep raw foods away from ready to eat foods. If you are cooking raw meats, make sure you have two dishes available to put food on. Use one for the raw meats and put the cooked meats in a separate dish once they are done and ready to eat. Food-borne illness, also known as food poisoning, is a digestive infection caused by eating contaminated food. This means keeping your meat thermometer cleaned after and before every use. Otherwise, you may transfer bacteria from one source to another.

Properly cook your meat until it is done. Heating and cooking your meat to 300° to 400° Fahrenheit kills bacteria. Use the thermometer to verify they have been heated at the desired temperature. Boil marinades before serving. When you marinate food, don't marinate it on the counter at room temperature. Room temperature is a good temperature and motivator for bacteria to reproduce. Put it in the refrigerator to marinate. Try not to reuse what's leftover in the marinades. You may be transferring the bacteria again.

Throw out leftovers within three or four days. You've heard the phrase, "When in doubt, throw it out." Use those words to your advantage. Defrost food safely. You can use the refrigerator to allow it to sit without having to expose it to room temperature and allowing bacteria to reproduce. Alternatively, you can use cold water or use the microwave. Just make sure the contents are sealed tightly. Now you are ready to indulge in these extraordinary super foods in a kitchen that is virtually bacteria-free and ready for warm bodies to soak up its comforting, wholesome, and delectable surroundings.

CHAPTER 9

LIBERATING YOURSELF
FROM SUGAR ADDICTION

There's an old adage that says: "You are what you eat." If that is true then Americans are the sweetest people in the world. As bizarre as it may seem, studies show that the average person in the United States eats 153 pounds of sugar a year. That's about ½ cup per day! This is done in spite of the fact that there is mounting scientific evidence that proves too much sugar is bad for you. Our internal systems are certainly not designed to digest the enormous amounts of sugar we are putting into our bodies.

Sugar addiction is a popular term describing a situation where individuals crave sweet foods and find them impossible to give up. There is clearly an aspect of emotional dependency that cannot be denied but recent research has identified elements of a physical addiction that is extremely difficult to overcome.

The idea that sugar is bad for us goes against our basic instincts. Our desire to eat something sweet helped us survive in the wild by driving us away from poisonous, bitter foods and toward beneficial natural foods like corn, peas, carrots, and fruit. As civilization evolved, we fell prey to the "more is better" theory and decided to put sugar into virtually everything. Sugar makes refined unhealthy foods taste good so we are drawn to them. In fact, we crave them much like an alcoholic craves a drink.

Elizabeth Bohorquez, RN and personal development hypnotherapist at Sarasota Medical Center, has conducted extensive research on sugar addiction. "Like all addictions, sugar addiction plays out in our mind and body. Sugar is very connected to emotional management including anxiety, panic disorder, depression, and a host of others. To understand why this is so, we have to become educated in the workings of food and beverage and relationships of family and personal medical history."

Most food manufacturers are well aware of the addictive qualities of sucrose, but almost all of them use it in food production. Studies conducted by the United States Department of Agriculture show that sugar consumption is increasing steadily every year. Most of the sugar we consume comes from cane, beet sugar, and corn syrup.

The major culprit in the increasing sugar intake appears to be the huge consumption of soft drinks, especially among children and teenagers. The evidence showing that soft drinks are major components of teen mood swings as well as child and adolescent obesity is so convincing that some lawmakers are crafting legislation designed at banning soft drinks and vending machines in public school settings.

Susan Burke, vice president of nutritional services for eDiet.com, puts it this way: "Just talking about how much sugar is in a can of soda is less effective than visualizing it. One 12-ounce can contains about 9 teaspoons of added sugar. That's about a quarter cup. It's also about 150 empty calories. The average American drinks almost two of these each day so he or she is getting nearly a half-cup of sugar from soft drinks. Imagine spooning 18 teaspoons of sugar from the sugar bowl into a big glass of club soda, then adding a couple of drops of food coloring ... would you drink it?"

A study conducted in Norway in the summer of 2006 concluded that Oslo teens that drank the most sugary drinks had more mental health problems such as hyperactivity and anxiety. Many scientists have come to refer to soft drinks as "liquid candy," and there is growing concern that the childhood obesity epidemic is closely related to soft drink consumption.

Obesity in childhood is a very serious matter and can lead to a host of medical problems including high cholesterol, hypertension, respiratory infections, and sleep apnea. Researchers report that impaired glucose tolerahce and insulin resistance are highly prevalent in children and adolescents who are overweight.

While not all sugar-addicted individuals are overweight, many are or will be if they continue to live their lives without dietary changes. Let's face it, most of us eat candy bars and chocolate cake in ADDITION to, not INSTEAD of, healthy food. So the calories just keep on climbing.

So what does this mean to you and your family? Obviously you can't follow your family around at work or school all day to monitor what they eat or drink, but you can instill sound nutritional values in them. And you can keep sugar out of your family's kitchen. Here are some simple things you can do to get started:

- Eliminate soft drinks from your refrigerator and replace them with healthy smoothies, flavored water (the extract of orange, lemon, and berries can really enhance the flavor of water; add 1 drop for every quart of purified water) and freshly squeezed juice (my family loves limeade made with fresh lemon, lime, and stevia, which is a sugar-free drink). Jazz up plain or sparkling water with fresh mint, a slice of lemon, or a splash of fruit juice.

- Keep store-bought "snacks" out of your kitchen and replace them with fruit, whole grain muffins, and nuts. Keep your "cookie" jar filled with bite-size pieces of whole grain nut/dried fruit bars.
- Get rid of white refined sugar and replace with agave syrup (rated a19 (low) on the Glycemic index), stevia (natural sugar-free substitute), raw cane sugar, or raw honey. Choose whole grain cereals that have no more than 8 grams of sugar per serving and that is made without corn syrup.
- Keep some fresh fruits or pre-cut vegetables readily available in the refrigerator so that family members can reach for them if they get "between meal" hunger pangs.
- Purchase a couple of cookbooks containing healthy recipes. Get the whole family involved in choosing their favorite recipes from the books and shopping for healthy ingredients.

Sugar in its natural form can be rich in minerals and vitamins. Refined sugar, on the other hand, has zero nutrients and acts more like a drug than a food. It quickly passes through the stomach, causing blood sugar levels to rise, then falls sharply. Once the plummet occurs, blood sugar levels drop to below normal. This condition is sometimes referred to as the "sugar blues." Symptoms of sugar blues include lethargy, depression, and irritability.

Refined sugar enters the bloodstream very rapidly, causing and contributing to a host of health problems and creating the perfect conditions for addiction. It aggravates many chronic diseases like pre-diabetes, heart and circulatory disorders, gastrointestinal disturbances including irritable bowel syndrome, GERD as well as PMS. Excessive sugar intake has also been linked to sleeping disorders.

If you ask baby boomers or seniors what their two most common complaints are, they say fatigue and pain. An elevated blood sugar level contributes to both. It prematurely ages the cells. Excessive sugar drains energy and it is particularly serious for people who have sensitive blood sugar responses. It's important to understand the impact sugar has on you and the dependency you have on it. Until you understand that, you will never get past it.

A recent report commissioned by the World Health Organization and the Food and Agriculture Organization suggested that sugar should not account for more than 10% of a healthy diet. Many individual foods provide large fractions of the USDA's recommended sugar limits. For instance, a typical cup of fruit yogurt provides 70% of a day's worth of added sugar; a cup of regular ice cream provides 60%, a 12-ounce soft drink provides 103%, and a quarter-cup of pancake syrup provides 103%.

The Center for Science in the Public Interest has studied the adverse effects of sugar for years. The center suggests the following tips to help liberate you from sugar addiction:

- Check food labels for sugar and its equivalents, including sucrose, high-fructose corn syrup, dextrose, glucose, honey, and molasses.

- Limit candy, cookies, cakes, pies, doughnuts, pastries, and other sweet baked foods. Eat fruit instead.

- Watch out for sweets served in restaurants (ice cream, shakes, and pastries); their huge servings can often provide a day's worth of added sugar and vast amounts of calories.

- Experiment with recipes that contain little or no sugar. Have fun with this. Healthy food does not have to be "boring" food.

- Try preparing your favorite recipes with much less sugar than you have traditionally used. You may be surprised at the tasty results.

The symptoms of sugar withdrawal can include headaches, fatigue, depression, drowsiness, skin eruptions, and throat discomfort. Let's face it, we're surrounded by the sweet stuff. Almost every packaged food or convenience project we see is made from sugar (or white flour which is actually very similar). Getting off the sweet stuff won't be easy, but you can do it. You didn't become addicted to sugar overnight, and you won't become "unaddicted" overnight either.

Make it easy on yourself. If you decide to kick the sugar habit, eat plenty of fruits and raw vegetables so that you feel satisfied and will have a better shot at staying off sugar for good.

Although eliminating sugar may seem difficult at first, the eventual rewards are great for your body, mind, and your taste buds. Once sugar is eliminated from the diet, all foods start to taste better. Taste buds become more sensitive to the natural sweetness of foods. Soon sugar cravings will be reduced. You'll feel better, look better, and sleep better. Sounds like a pretty sweet deal.

CHAPTER 10

HOW TO READ
FOOD LABELS

Repeatedly you have heard, "Watch what you eat." Even in this book, I have told you over and over about the importance of watching what you eat. You are what you eat, so you have to be cautious about what you put into your body. Do you believe your body is a garbage disposal or your temple? Reading the labels on products you buy gets you going in the right direction. How do I decipher food labels? Aren't they written in hieroglyphics? Generally, no.

Food labels are easier to read than you think. To read a food label, know the direction the information is presented and the important information that you are looking for. Read labels from top to bottom. The facts presented on packages are listed by serving size. The serving size is the first bit of information listed on the information label. It may not equal the actual serving size of the total package, but the calories and nutrients are listed per serving size.

Next, the servings per package will be listed under the serving size. If the serving per package is one, then everything contained in that box is equal to the amount of calories and fats you will consume by eating the entire package. If the servings per package are larger than one, then multiply all the information listed below by that number to get a more accurate description of the contents in the box.

If you are counting calories, the next section of the label lists the calories and the calories from fat. All fats are not evil, but you still want to pay close attention to this section if your goal is to lose weight.

FDA guidelines for Calories:
40 calories is low
100 calories is moderate
400 or more calories is high

Then, find listed the information on the fats, saturated fats, trans fats, cholesterol, and sodium. These are the items that we are having trouble with. We are getting plenty, and in most cases, too much. Good fats aid in the absorption of vitamins, are sources of energy, and help the stomach feel full. Trans fats and saturated fats increase your risk of heart disease, some cancers, and high blood pressure.

Just below the fats are the vitamins. These are the things that we are not getting enough of and the stuff that little girls and boys need plenty of to become healthy big boys and girls.

The footnote of the label does not pertain to the specific product. It is a recommendation to the average American that if you are counting calories, then this is the amount of fats, cholesterol's, etc. you can consume today to meet your calories count.

Lastly, the percent daily value based on the serving size helps determine if a product is high or low in certain nutrients.

FDA guideline:
5% low
20% high

Another very important element of reading food labels is reading the ingredient list. This time I must admit that most of the boxed and quick food items are written in hieroglyphics. Remember the 12,000 food additives we talked about in the previous chapter. Well you'll be sure to find most of these ingredients in the center isle of the grocery store. So if you want to stick with whole foods, try to stay in the outer isles where you'll find most, if not all, of your whole foods virtually free of preservatives, fillers, binders, additives, and artificial coloring and flavorings.

CHAPTER 11

EXTENDING THE SHELF LIFE OF PERISHABLE FOOD

Perishable foods are defined as foods not stable at room temperature and require cool, cold, or colder storage for longevity. Alternatively, it can also be defined as the length of time that corresponds to a tolerable loss in quality of a processed food. Spoilage organisms like bacteria and fungus reduce product shelf life. There organisms reproduce more of themselves and increase the deterioration of food. If you eat these infected foods, then you have just ingested bacteria. Unfortunately, most of them will make you sick, some seriously ill.

Food spoilage is measured by the growth of microorganisms and by the rate of its chemical changes. Perishable foods include fruits, foods from frozen sections of grocery stores, pre-cooked foods, vegetables, and fresh meat. Most cross-contamination of fresh produce occurs during cold storage. Leaving infected fruit in batches with other fruits opens the door to spreading the viruses. Throw them all out. Eating them will only make you sick. The following chart will help you stay mindful of the expiration date of your perishables:

Food	Shelf Life In Refrigerator
Milk	5-7 days
Cream	5 days
Cheese	variable (1-3 months)
Eggs	3-6 weeks
Butter	8 weeks
Oil and fat	variable (6 months)
Seafood	3 days
Meat	3-5 days
Minced meat	2-3 days
Cured meat	2-3 weeks
Poultry	3 days
Fresh Fruit and its juices	7-14 days
Vegetables	7-14 days

Many have successfully used vacuum packaging as protection against mold and food viruses. Vacuum packaging does help to eliminate growth of spoilage bacteria. Oxygen deteriorates the quality of food. However, without the competition of spoilage bacteria, pathogens produce more rapidly from the lack of competition once opened. Therefore, it is best to use the food that has been vacuum-sealed immediately upon opening. Also, consider bringing a cooler with you when doing major grocery shopping a distance away from home. It can be very helpful in terms of preserving your perishables from going bad or protect it from heat exposure in your trunk.

PREPARING YOUR KITCHEN FOR STORAGE

Always defrost your refrigerator regularly. Check the temperature in the fridge to ensure it is working properly. Refrigerate packaged foods at 38° to 42° Fahrenheit. When you plan to thaw foods, use the refrigerator instead of allowing them to sit out in the open to thaw. Don't crowd the refrigerator. Separating and having space in your refrigerator reduces the risks of cross-contamination.

At the grocery store, buy only refrigerated perishables and make those the last items you put in your cart on the shopping trip. You don't want to get them first, have them sitting in your cart under room temperature and starting to thaw, resulting in deterioration before you get out of the store. Unwrap and wash chicken when you get home and unpack the groceries. Also, gut and clean fresh fish immediately. Re-wrap it, and then freeze it. Amazingly, unwrapped meats last longer than wrapped meats. They are not pretty to look at after a while, but the hard crusts the meats form on the top of them actually protects them from bacteria longer.

Remember to read the safe handling instructions of foods if available. If there are "use by dates" stamped on your grocery items, please adhere to those dates.

Now that you plan to eat more nutrient-dense whole foods, it's equally important to eat them while they're fresh for the best flavor and nutrition. Remember, natural foods contain no chemical preservatives, so their shelf life is shorter than refined products. Almost half of all food is wasted in America, so remember to develop good shopping and storage habits to help reduce unnecessary waste.

STORING WHOLE FOODS

- Keep all unrefined oils in the refrigerator with the exception of olive oil. Unrefined oils turn rancid quickly at warm temperatures.

- Whole grains in unbroken kernels (such as whole grains of wheat, rye, millet, corn, and oats) may be kept in tightly covered mason jars in your cabinet or pantry. Whole grains that have been cracked, rolled, or ground into flour, meal, or flakes should be refrigerated or frozen because the oils that they contain gradually go rancid when exposed to oxygen. Brown rice should also be kept cool because its oils are in the bran layer, near the surface of the grain.

- Dried beans and legumes can be stored in a cool, dry place for many months without loss of nutritional value. However, they will become dry the longer they sit around and, hence, take longer to cook. Remember to soak your beans overnight (minimum 8 hours) before cooking. Doing so will release the enzyme inhibitors and increase your ability to digest it. In addition, adding dried sea vegetables (like kelp or dulse) to the water can increase the mineral content of your beans.

- Cooked beans and grains will keep in the refrigerator for about one week if they are seasoned with sea salt. Sea salt is a natural preservative and helps prolong the life of leftovers. Cooked beans and grains can also be frozen.

- Nuts, seeds, and their butters also contain oils and should be kept refrigerated unless you're using them daily. In order to increase assimilation of your nuts (i.e. almonds, cashew, walnuts, etc.), soak them for at least 4 hours, drain, and let dry. Your nuts will be plump, delicious, and extremely digestible.

- If you buy bulk herbs and spices in small bags, transfer them to glass mason jars with tight-fitting lids when you get home and keep them away from light and heat. Otherwise, they will quickly lose their flavor. They also lose flavor over time, so only buy as much as you need.

- Whole grain breads and baked goods that do not contain preservatives also need to be refrigerated, or better yet, frozen, if you are not using them right away. Frozen bread lasts longer, will not mold, and you can take just what you need from the bag without having to defrost the entire loaf. Your bread will taste fresh and thaws quite well in the toaster.

STORING AND RIPENING FRUITS

Most fruit (including avocados and tomatoes) should be stored at room temperature until ripe. Exceptions to these are berries, grapes, fresh figs, melons, pineapple, coconut, and tangerines, which can be stored and refrigerated in mason jars. A handheld food saver can remove the oxygen from your mason jar and increase the shelf life by 3 or 4 days longer. Apples can also be refrigerated or stored in a cool dark place.

To speed ripening, place fruit in a loosely closed paper bag. Leave at room temperature, out of direct sunlight. The paper bag holds in ethylene, a gas produced naturally by the fruit, which helps speed up the ripening process. Don't use a plastic container as it traps moisture and air, which causes spoilage. Once ripe, eat fruits right away. You can also refrigerate ripe fruits for a few days, but keep them separate from other vegetables, as the ethylene gas they emit can speed decay.

STORING VEGETABLES

Most vegetables should be stored in the refrigerator. A cold temperature slows respiration, but you don't want to stop the breathing completely. Place items loosely in the crisper or in open bags to allow breathing. Consider the Evert-Fresh green vegetable and fruit bag that uses revolutionary technology to preserve freshness and to prolong the life of fruits, vegetables, and cut flowers without chemicals. These special bags provide your produce with the following benefits:

* Absorbs and removes damaging gases: Most fruit, vegetables, and flowers release damaging gases during the natural ripening process after harvest. Exposure of the produce to these gases accelerates aging and ultimate deterioration. Evert-Fresh bags remove these gases to prolong the life and freshness of produce.

* Moisture barrier: Evert-Fresh bags are manufactured to reduce moisture build-up inhibiting bacteria, fungus, mold, and decay.
  Don't overcrowd. "The worst thing you can do is seal too many fruits and vegetables in airtight bags," says Barry Swanson, professor of food science and human nutrition at Washington State University. Mushrooms should be brushed with a soft fruit and vegetable brush of peat or soil, stored, and refrigerated in paper bags.

Don't wash fresh fruits and vegetables before storing. Fresh produce has a natural protective coating that keeps in moisture and freshness. Washing and scrubbing will damage the coating and speed up spoilage. Produce will last longer when it is whole. When shopping, look for greens that have some of the stem intact. Don't buy prepared salad greens or veggies unless you plan on using them that day. At home, don't chop veggies and store for later use.

Root veggies such as beets, carrots, and radishes can be purchased with their greens. For these items, cut off the greens once you get home to prevent the roots from going soft. Radish and beet greens taste good in soup. For greens, cut off elastic bands and damaged leaves before refrigerating. Inspect your greens daily and remove any wilting leaves. Check your other produce and remove any rotting items immediately. One bad apple can spoil the bunch.
Don't refrigerate garlic, cooking onions, winter squash, and potatoes. These items can be stored uncovered in a dark cool place, but try to use them within a week or two before they begin to rot. Fresh ginger will keep for up to a couple of weeks in the fridge in a paper bag. Ginger also freezes well, either whole or grated. One of the best ways to store ginger is to bury it in a small clay pot filled with sand. Some vegetables can be stored for several months in a root cellar if certain criteria are met. The ideal cold storage room must be dry, dark, and cool (7°C to 10°C). Basements, garages, and cupboards in today's homes are often not equipped to meet these three conditions.

TOTAL NUTRITION KITCHEN MAKEOVER™

CHAPTER 12

HERBS, HERBS AND MORE HERBS

Herbs are plants or plant parts we value for their medicinal qualities. Like anything else, if you have an interest in using herbal supplements, research the herb thoroughly before you start using it. Since herbs come from plants, verify that you are not allergic to the plants before you begin using the herb extracted from it.

Herbs and supplements are available in drugstores, health food stores, grocery stores, on the Internet, from practitioners, and by mail order. Go to a reliable health food store, drugstore, or grocery store that will refund a product if there are problems. The Internet doesn't offer the chance to see the product and scrutinize the label before you buy it.

Do not buy the cheapest because these are often the products that are examined in the studies comparing the amount stated on the label to the actual amount in the bottle, and they have been found to contain little or nothing. If price is a concern, buy somewhere in the middle range. Remember the rule, you get what you pay for. Herbs come in many forms: capsules, teas, tablets, etc. The amount of alcohol in the mixture depends on the herb. And physicians believe most people absorb alcohol extracts best. Some manufacturers will remove some of the alcohol in order to make the mixture more palatable.

Capsules are plant extracts that have been dried and ground up. The taste of an herb in tea form may not be your thing, but a capsule can give you the same benefits. People with strong digestive systems can digest the capsule shell, but older people and people with low stomach acid secretion and poor digestion may have some difficulty. The amount of each ingredient in the capsule should be listed on the label and tell how much of each herb the capsule contains.

Tea is a staple in many cultures outside of the United States. The secret to getting the essential elements when brewing tea is to make sure your kettle or pot is covered to trap the oils inside. Some herbal teas can be grown at home as touted by Sean Paajanen, the tea guru. The following represents a growing list of teas that many cultures enjoy and can benefit from both therapeutically and for relaxation purposes. Instructions are provided so you can grow them at home:

Herbs for Tea

Mint
Mint is well known for its ability to sooth the digestive tract and reduces the severity and length of stomach aches. In addition, mint teas and other herbal preparations have shown great promise at easing the discomfort associated with irritable bowel syndrome and even at slowing the growth of many of the most harmful bacteria and fungi. The well-documented antifungal properties of mint are thought to play a role in the treatment of asthma and many allergy conditions as well.

Mint tea is a favorite among herbal tea drinkers and is one of the easiest to grow yourself. The plant is very hardy and may even get out of control in the garden unless you take care to contain it. Mint should get at least a partial day of good sun, but all-day sun might be too much for it. Make sure to water well during the peak of summer heat. There are many varieties to choose from, each with its own unique taste: spearmint, peppermint, apple mint, or even chocolate mint. Mint will grow readily indoors.

Chamomile
Chamomile may reduce intestinal cramping and ease the irritation and inflammation associated with diarrhea. Chamomile is typically drunk as a tea; many doctors recommend dissolving 2–3 grams of powdered chamomile or adding 3–5mL of a chamomile liquid extract to hot water and drinking it three or more times per day between meals. Chamomile tea is made with the small white and yellow flowers of the chamomile plant, rather than the leaves. There are two kinds of chamomile (German and Roman) and it's the German variety that makes the best tea. Chamomile likes sandy soils and lots of sun, but you'll need to give it plenty of water during the hottest parts of the summer. Though technically an annual, chamomile goes to seed so readily that you will likely see it every year in your garden. You can grow chamomile in containers on a balcony, but it doesn't do well indoors.

Lemon Balm
Lemon balm can be compared with the effectiveness of mint in the soothing effect it has on the stomach and the positive effect it has on the digestive system. Lemon balm is used to relieve pain and discomfort associated with indigestion and offers relief for such symptoms as gas and bloating. Lemon balm is also beneficial to those suffering from nervousness, anxiety, and slight insomnia. Lemon balm helps to calm and relax the nerves and has been used successfully since the Middle Ages.

The lemon balm plant is actually closely related to mint but has a distinct lemon aroma. It likes somewhat dry soil and partial shade during the day. Besides making a nice herbal tea, you can also use lemon balm as a spice when cooking (I like it with fish). Like its minty cousin, you can grow lemon balm indoors.

Rose Hips
Rose hips will make a nicely citrus-tasting tea that is rich in Vitamin C. Any rose plant will create "hips," but Rugosa roses produce the largest ones. The hips are actually seed pods that form at the base of the rose blooms. When making tea with dried rose hips, you should slice them in half before steeping. You may want to remove the seeds before making your tea, but it's not necessary. If you do choose to de-seed your hips, do so before you dry them. Rugosa roses are hardy and cold-tolerant. They grow in bushes between 2' to 6' tall. These roses will grow just about anywhere, but they aren't really suitable for a windowsill garden.

Lavender
Lavender makes a lovely addition to any garden, even if you're not using it for tea. Lavender will grow 2 or 3 feet tall, which makes it inappropriate for a windowsill, but can easily be grown on the balcony in containers. Your soil should be well-drained, and lavender likes plenty of direct sun. Some lavender varieties take the cold better than others. You might not think of lavender for tea, but it makes for a floral-tasting tea that also blends well with other herbs (like chamomile).

Fennel
Fennel is helpful in colic, protects the liver from toxins, and has a slight pain-reducing potential in dysmenorrhea (painful menstrual cramps). There are several kinds of fennel, but the type typically grown for tea use is the sweet fennel. When dried, the seeds have a very strong licorice flavor. Unlike the other herbs, you don't really harvest fennel periodically through the summer. The plant will go to seed at the end of summer or start of fall. You can let the seed dry right on the plant and then collect for tea. You won't want to grow fennel indoors because it can grow up to 6 feet tall. Also, don't plant it next to its close relative, dill, because they can cross-pollinate. Fennel likes lots of sun and lots of water.

Peppermint
Peppermint tea is usually a combination of tea and peppermint or an infusion of peppermint alone. Considered to have many of the same health benefits as mint, it is a much sought after tea in the market today. To prepare a cup of peppermint tea, pour boiling water over dried peppermint leaves and leave for ten minutes. Alternatively, simply add boiling water to peppermint

tea bags and allow it to stand for 2-3 minutes.

Camellia Sinensis (Green Tea)
Today, scientific research in both Asia and the West is providing hard evidence for the many health benefits associated with drinking green tea. For example, in 1994 the Journal of the National Cancer Institute published the results of an epidemiological study that indicated drinking green tea reduces the risk of esophageal cancer in Chinese men and women by nearly 60%. University of Purdue researchers recently concluded that a compound in green tea inhibits the growth of cancer cells. There is also research indicating that drinking green tea lowers total cholesterol levels, as well as improving the ratio of good (HDL) cholesterol to bad (LDL) cholesterol.

The whole leaves and buds are used to produce the health-enhancing and curative benefits of Camellia Sinensis. Different types of tea such as white, green, oolong, and so on are harvested from Camellia but are processed differently to attain different levels of oxidation. Different leaf ages produce different tea qualities; fresh leaves contain about 4% caffeine.

Valerian
Valerian is a hardy perennial flowering plant with heads of sweetly scented pink or white flowers. In the past, Valerian was recommended as a sedative; the main use of Valerian today is a remedy for insomnia. When preparing Valerian tea, use warm water rather than boiling water, as boiling water drives off lighter oils.

Herbs for Cooking and Preparing Food

Fenugreek
Fenugreek is used both as an herb and as a spice. The yellow fenugreek seed is frequently used in the preparation of pickles, and curry powders and pastes, which are characteristic of Indian and Thai cuisine. Young fresh leaves and sprouts are eaten as greens while dried or fresh leaves are used for flavoring dishes.

Thyme
Thyme is a genus of about 350 species of aromatic perennial herbs and subshrubs native to Europe, North Africa, and Asia. Common thyme is a commonly used culinary herb whereas Caraway thyme is used as both a culinary herb and a groundcover. Thyme is commonly used to flavor meats, soups, and stews. While cooking, it is advised that thyme be added early to allow time for release of oils.

Savory

Savory is best known for flavoring beans and is often cultivated for uses such as potherbs. It is an annual plant with small green leaves and pink flowers. Savory is commonly used in the traditional Acadian stew, fricot, as a seasoning. They are low-growing plants found in dry sunny regions and range from 15 to 50 cms in height. Flowers are produced in whorls and range from white to pale pink-violet in color.

Cilantro

Cilantro is also commonly known as coriander and is native to southwestern Asia to North Africa. It is a soft hairless plant that grows to 50 cms. in height. All parts of Cilantro are edible, with fresh leaves and dried seeds being the most common. Fresh Cilantro herb is best stored in the refrigerator in airtight containers after removal of roots.

Rosemary

Rosemary is a woody perennial herb with fragrant evergreen leaves. It is a member of the mint family. Fresh and dried leaves are used frequently in traditional Mediterranean cooking. The leaves are evergreen and range from 2 to 4 cm in length. They are broad in shape with green coloring on top and white below with dense hairs. Flowers are variable in color being pink, white, purple, or blue.

Dill Weed

Dill is a short-lived annual herb native to Europe, North Africa, and Asia. Its fernlike leaves are aromatic and are used to flavor many foods such as pickled salmon, soups, and other pickles. Seeds are also commonly used in pickles. Dill leaves must be used fresh as they lose their flavor when dried or frozen.

Tarragon

Tarragon is another perennial herb native to the Northern Hemisphere. French Tarragon is the most commonly used culinary variety and is particularly suitable for fish and chicken dishes. Another common culinary variety, not as flavorful or aromatic as the French, is the Russian tarragon.

Oregano

Oregano is the most popular culinary herb used today. It is particularly used in Greek and Italian cuisines. Most common dishes that use Oregano are fried vegetables, tomato sauce, and grilled meat. Oregano can also be added to Greek salads, lemon-olive oil sauce, casseroles, and fish barbecues. It has a distinct aroma with a warm but slightly bitter taste and varies in intensity.

Turmeric
Turmeric is a commonly used spice for curries and South Asian cuisine. It is a significant ingredient in curry powders and gives a yellow color to prepared meals such as chicken broth. It is a member of the ginger family and has many healthful properties.

Sweet Basil
Basil is a low-growing herb native to tropical Asia. For culinary purposes, it is recommended that basil be used fresh and is generally added in the last moment during cooking, as heat destroys its flavor. It can be stored in the refrigerator for a short while or for longer durations in the freezer after quickly blanching in boiling water. Basil is most commonly used in fresh fruit, fruit jams, and sauces.

Storing and Preserving the Integrity of your Tea
Although each type of tea has a different shelf life, it is best when used within 6 to 12 months of purchase. Green teas perish the fastest and deteriorate within a year of harvest. Oolong and black teas preserve their characteristics for several years.

Keep your loose-leaf teas stored in a cool, dark place to preserve their freshness and avoid exposure to light. Always store your teas in opaque jars with airtight lids.

Another factor contributing to a tea's life span is the way in which the tea-leaf is rolled. Tea leaves that are rolled into pellets or twisted last longer than an open, flat leafs because less of their surface area is exposed to air. Whichever tea you choose, remember to care for it as you would a delicate spice. Keep it away from heat, moisture, and other strongly scented teas or spices.

Starting a family tea tradition

The art of drinking and serving tea plays a major cultural role in China. It inspires poetry and songs. Mutual love of tea cements lifelong friendships. For centuries, the ritual of preparing and serving tea has held a special place in the hearts and minds of Chinese aristocracy, court officials, intellectuals, and poets.

The Chinese tea ceremony emphasizes the tea, rather than the ceremony. However, a tea tradition in your home can provide an intimate space where family members can feel safe to share their concerns of life. To begin your tea tradition, you will need the following wares placed unobtrusively in your recreation or living room area (choose a place your family spends the most time other than the kitchen).

- A small wooden serving table with at least 2 shelves

- An electric tea kettle (Hamilton Beach sells a cordless version—Proctor Silex)

- Ornate ceramic tea cups

- A rectangular wicker, wooden, metal, or plastic box

- An assortment of teas that come in individually wrapped bags

- Agave or stevia sweetener

- Stirrers w/ dispenser

- Small serving napkins

- Individually wrapped Organic Biscotti Almond Cookies (optional)

- A small vase containing 1 or 2 exotic flowers

Once you've decided on the location of your tea station, fill your tea kettle with filtered water and place it on the left or right side of your table, set the vase on the other side towards the back and your ceramic tea cups in the front. The remaining items can be placed on the lower shelves. Be sure to fill your box with the assortment of teas you've purchased. It's a good idea to remove all of the individually wrapped tea bags from the box they came in and place them row by row in your rectangular container. Make sure your box can easily be accessed unencumbered. Plug your electric tea kettle into your outlet, and if you decided to purchase the Proctor Silex, all you have to do is push down the lever and in a few seconds your family will have hot water ready for the ceremony. What an awesome way to calmly bring the family together!

CHAPTER 13

GOING ORGANIC

Not long ago, human excrements were used to fertilize our food. Add that to pesticides and herbicides and you may consider going completely organic with your new diet. If that were not enough to change your mind, maybe you prefer having hormones, antibiotics, and remains of other animals injected into your meat. These drugs are passed directly onto the consumers of their dairy produce or meat, which must be a contributing factor to meat-related diseases like coronaries and high blood pressure.

It does not stop with the meats. Did you know that the spices we use from regular grocery stores are placed under radiation to kill bacteria? It sounds like a great idea to kill the bacteria before it gets in my mouth, so now the only thing I have to worry about are the long-term side effects of the radiation on my internal organs. The average conventionally grown apple has 20-30 artificial poisons on its skin, even after rinsing. Organic foods reduce the amount of cancer-causing chemicals we take into our body. From organic meats come healthier cows, chickens, and other animals. You can make a statement about your body and the importance of physical health when you buy organic food. You also help protect the environment when you take money away from pesticide companies and farmers who use means that can later destroy organs in your body. Intensive farming can seriously damage farm workers' health. There are much higher instances of cancer, respiratory problems, and other major diseases in farm workers from non-organic farms. We spend billions of pounds every year cleaning up the mess that agro-chemicals create in our natural water supply.

There are many so-called foods that claim to be organic, but many of them don't deserve the label. To be considered organically grown, one must use little to no synthetic fertilizers and/or pesticides. Organic food is good to eat, good for the environment, and good for small-scale farmers. Not to mention the fact that there is an inherent difference in the way an organic tomato tastes versus its conventional counterpart. The food seems to be more flavorful, juicier, and richer in color and ripens quite well. Just the opposite is true with conventionally grown produce which increases your risk to illness.

Chemotherapy patients are advised to eat only organic and whole food products because their bodies cannot cope with the chemical additives that are often associated to a suppressed immunologic function. Fresh organic produce contains on average 50% more vitamins, minerals, enzymes, and other micro-nutrients than intensively farmed produce.

The Organic Trade Association suggests several reasons you should switch to organic foods. "Organic certification is the public's assurance that products have been grown and handled according to strict procedures without persistent toxic chemical inputs. Well-balanced soils produce strong, healthy plants that become nourishing food for people and animals. Organic agriculture is one way to prevent any more of these chemicals from getting into the air, earth, and water that sustain us.

The elimination of polluting chemicals and nitrogen leaching, done in combination with soil building, protects and conserves water resources. Soil is the foundation of the food chain. The primary focus of organic farming is to use practices that build healthy soils. Organic agriculture respects the balance demanded of a healthy ecosystem: wildlife is encouraged by including forage crops in rotation and by retaining fence rows, wetlands, and other natural areas.

Organic farmers have led the way, largely at their own expense, with innovative on-farm research aimed at reducing pesticide use and minimizing agriculture's impact on the environment. The loss of a large variety of species (biodiversity) is one of the most pressing environmental concerns. The good news is that many organic farmers and gardeners have been collecting and preserving seeds and growing unusual varieties for decades."

The USDA reported that in 1997 half of U.S. farm production came from only 2% of farms. Organic agriculture can be a lifeline for small farms because it offers an alternative market where sellers can command fair prices for crops. Now every food category has an organic alternative. There are more places that you can go to find organic foods today than ten years ago. The first place to start is your local supermarket. Many supermarkets carry some organic produce and packaged foods now. If we collectively create even more of a demand than there is currently, conventional supermarkets may have to re-consider the sources of their products.

Natural food stores, like Whole Foods, offer a wide variety of organic foods. Look for smaller, independent, locally owned stores, which often buy organic produce directly from local farms. Farmers markets connect us directly with local farmers and are conscientious about how the food is grown. There are more than 2,400 farmers markets across the country, according to the USDA. The majority feature organic and conventional produce that is grown locally.

Food co-ops, or buying clubs, allow consumers to purchase food in bulk directly from farmers and other suppliers, usually at wholesale prices. Some co-ops occupy a permanent site, such as a storefront or garage. The best benefit of organic foods is that you don't have to buy it from the store. You can grow many of your own food. Home Depot offers classes on how to start a home garden for a minimal fee. Oftentimes, they offer free classes to encourage customers to come into the stores and buy from them. If you live in an apartment, you are not limited. You can have a windowsill vegetable garden. You can buy these at Home Depot or other hardware stores as well. Don't be afraid to ask the salesperson for tips on getting started.

OK, you're really excited about becoming an organic food convert but have just one minor hurdle to overcome: you don't typically eat fresh fruits and vegetables. So you probably don't know where to begin. Don't worry; you're not alone. The average person who eats the SAD (Standard American Diet) eats less than 4 servings of both fruits and vegetable per day. (The USDA's minimum requirement is 9 in order to be healthy and prevent such diseases as cancer, diabetes and hypertension.)

Following is a basic list of fresh fruits and vegetables. You'll learn what they're good for, when they're in season, how to pick them at the supermarket, and how they're typically prepared or eaten:

Fruits
- Fruit Nutrition Facts

Fruit	Calories	Carb. gm.	Fiber gm.	Potassium mg.	Vitamin A	Vitamin C	Calcium	Iron
					\multicolumn{4}{c}{% Daily Value}			
Apple, 1 med. (154 g.)	80	22	5	170	2	8	*	2
Avocado, 1/2 med.	140	8	8	430	*	10	*	*
Banana, 1 med.	110	29	4	400	*	15	*	2
Blackberries, 1 cup, raw	70	18	8	280	4	50	4	4
Blueberries, 1 cup, raw	80	20	4	130	2	30	*	*
Boysenberries, 1 cup, raw	70	18	8	280	4	50	4	4
Cantaloupe, 1/2 med.	100	23	2	850	180	190	4	4
Casaba, 1 cup, cubed	45	11	1	360	*	45	*	4

Cherimoya, 1 raw	250	66	6	n/a	*	40	8	8
Cherries, 1 cup, raw	90	22	3	300	2	15	2	2
Coconut, fresh, 50 g.	180	8	5	180	*	2	*	6
Cranberries (whole), 1 cup	45	12	4	65	*	20	*	*
Figs, 1 large, fresh	45	12	2	150	*	2	2	*
Grapes, 1 cup	60	16	<1	180	*	15	*	*
Grapefruit, 1/2 med.	60	16	6	230	15	110	2	*
Guava, 1 med.	45	11	5	260	15	280	*	*
Honeydew, 1/4 med.	130	33	3	780	6	110	*	6
Kiwifruit, 1 med.	50	12	2	240	*	120	4	2
Kumquat, 4 each	50	12	5	150	4	45	4	*
Lemon, 1 med.	15	5	1	90	*	40	2	*
Lime, 1 med.	20	7	2	75	*	35	*	*
Loquat, 1 large	10	2	n/a	55	6	*	*	*
Mandarin Orange, 1 large	45	11	2	150	20	50	*	*
Mango, 1 med. raw	130	35	4	320	160	100	2	*
Nectarine, 1 med. raw	70	16	2	300	4	15	*	2
Orange, 100 g.	45	14	5	170	*	80	4	*
Orange (Valencia), 100 g.	50	12	3	180	4	80	4	*
Papaya, 1 med.	120	30	5	780	15	310	8	*
Passion Fruit, 3 med.	50	13	6	190	8	25	*	4

Peach, 1 med.	40	11	2	190	2	10	*	*
Pear, 1 med.	100	25	4	210	*	10	2	*
Persimmon, 1 med.	30	8	n/a	80	*	30	*	4
Pineapple, 1 cup, diced	80	19	2	180	*	40	*	4
Plantain, 1 med.	220	57	4	890	40	50	*	6
Plum, 1 med.	40	10	1	110	4	10	*	*
Pomegranate, 1 med.	100	26	<1	400	*	15	*	2
Prickly Pear	40	10	4	230	*	25	6	*
Quince, 1 med.	50	14	2	180	*	25	*	4
Raspberries, 1 cup, fresh	60	14	8	190	4	50	2	4
Strawberries, 100 g. fresh	30	8	3	180	*	110	*	2
Tamarind 1/2 cup	140	38	3	380	*	4	4	10
Tangerine, 1 med.	50	15	3	180	*	50	4	*
Tangelo, 1 med.	60	15	3	240	6	120	6	*
Tomatillo, 1/2 cup diced, raw	20	4	1	180	*	15	*	2
Tomato, med. raw	35	7	1	360	20	40	2	2
Tomato (Cherry), 5 each, raw	20	4	<1	190	10	15	*	2
Tomato (Roma), 3 med. raw	40	9	2	410	25	60	*	4
Watermelon, 2 cups, diced	80	27	2	230	20	25	2	4

* Contains less than 2% Daily Value
Amounts given are approximations; nutritional content will vary slightly, depending on growing conditions, etc.

Apples
Apples have always been considered a healthy fruit. Today, research shows that apples reduce the risk of colon cancer, prostate cancer, and lung cancer. They contain a plethora of antioxidant compounds and Vitamin C. The fiber present in apples helps keep the bowels healthy. Apples are also excellent when preventing heart disease, trying for weight loss, and controlling cholesterol. A cooking apple is very different from a normal apple since it contains less sugar and it has a firmer flesh that does not break easily upon cooking. They can be served with custard, put in apple pie, baked in an oven, or as applesauce. When picking apples, try to avoid those that have brown spots or bruising.

Avocado
An excellent source of potassium, folic acid, and Vitamin C, avocados have very little sugar or starch; nevertheless, they include more protein than any other fruit. Their high oil content is 70% monounsaturated, much like olive oil. The soft tissue of avocados can be chopped along with tomatoes, cucumbers, and other vegetables for a delicious vegetable salsa or mix avocado with pineapple juice and cream cheese for a creamy dressing for fruit salad.
Depending on variety, avocados can be round or pear-shaped, purplish-brown or dark green, smooth and shiny or coarse and grainy. Size, shape, and color have little bearing on the quality of fruit.
Look for fruit that is clean and free of bruises or soft spots. Hass avocados are the most popular variety sold in North America, and are nearly black with gravel-like skin, and have a high fat content with relatively small pits. Avocados should preferably be eaten raw or prepared immediately before consumption, since cutting and exposure to the air darkens the flesh.

Berries
Berries, with their variety of flavor and benefits to health, occupy a unique place in our diet. These colorful fruits have high levels of antioxidants, and they have been shown to help with brain, eye, and vascular health. Antioxidants are compounds that protect cells from free radical damage. In addition, berries are also a good source of fiber.
Berries can be broadly divided into blackberries, blueberries, cranberries, gooseberries, raspberries, and strawberries. Each category offers distinctive properties and flavors, from healthful snacking to sophisticated desserts.

Blackberries
The blackberry is a bramble fruit, which grows on bushes with thorns. Like most dark-colored fruits, blackberries are rich in antioxidants, including vitamins C and E as well as ellagic acid.
Blackberries can be added to numerous recipes for desserts, jams, and drinks

and are available fresh, frozen, or canned. The prime season for fresh berries runs from May through September, crowning in June and July.

Fresh blackberries are the more difficult to find in-season than other berries because shipping hastens loss of quality. Locally grown berries sold are your best bet. When shopping for berries, look for those that are firm, dry, and of uniform purplish-black color.

Blueberries

Blueberries are native to North America and were an important Native American food. A tea is made from the leaves to revitalize the blood. Wild blueberries are the size of small peas whereas cultivated varieties are marble-sized and have fewer flavors. Because of their small size, wild blueberries yield more pulp and therefore contain more antioxidants than domesticated varieties. Today, blueberries, both wild and domestic, are increasingly recognized for their great health benefits.

The spell for blueberries stretches from May through October, peaking in July for U.S-grown berries. Imported berries are available at other times of the year. Select firm, dry berries that have a faint whitish bloom over a uniform blue-black color. The chalky bloom is a sign of freshness and should not be mistaken for mold. Gently shake the carton to make sure the berries move freely; this is an indication of proper freezing without the risk of defrosting and refreezing.

Cranberries

Also native to North America, cranberries are from the blueberry family. The health value of cranberries has grown due to a research study that showed the effectiveness of cranberries in reducing the incidence of urinary tract infections when ingested as juice. Cranberries are consumed as juice or sauce. The peak season for cranberries is from October through December. Firmness is the best indicator of quality, while depth of color is a measure of their antioxidant content. Fresh berries are sold hand-packed in containers or at farmer's markets.

Gooseberries

Related to the berry family, gooseberries are usually a pale translucent green to yellow to purplish red and are similar to small grapes in size. Sauces made from them harmonize well with game meats, especially roast goose. They can be consumed in pies, puddings, and a soufflé dessert called Gooseberry Fool. The gooseberry season runs from June to August, peaking in July. Early season gooseberries are the green varieties that are smaller and firmer than the late-season varieties. Late-season berries are larger and range in color from yellow to red, are sweeter, and can be eaten raw. When buying gooseberries, make sure that they are clean, plump, and feel like grapes.

Raspberries

Raspberries are fragile and elegant in both formation and taste, having a concave core and a sharper flavor. In spite of their fragility, raspberries are high in nutritional value and are filled with antioxidants and dietary fiber. Raspberries are most copious from May through October. When buying raspberries, be sure that they are plump, firm, dry, and deeply colored. Avoid berries that show mold, moisture, or loss of color, as these are spoilt and risky to eat.

Strawberries

Strawberries are second only to blueberries in their antioxidant content, although they have more Vitamin C than any other berry.

The strawberry season runs from the months of April to July. Always choose berries that are firm, dry, well-shaped, and display a uniform deep-red color. Medium-sized berries often have better flavor than extremely large ones, so don't get tempted to buy the biggest. Check cellophane-wrapped containers for stains or dampness, which could indicate damage to the fruit inside. Also, look under the top layer of berries in open containers to check for mold.

Caribbean Fruit

Citrus fruits such as lemons, limes, grapefruits, and oranges are commonly known as Caribbean fruit. Below is a description of each along with uses.

Guava

The small green- or yellow-colored fruit has a tough rind that protects the creamy white-pink flesh inside. Tiny seeds characterize guava.

Sweet, juicy, and extremely fragrant, the fruit is more often enjoyed raw.

Breadfruit

This grapefruit-sized fruit is green in color and has a roughly textured surface. Extremely versatile, breadfruit can be baked, broiled, roasted, or added to soups or other dishes. It can also be used like a potato, pairing it with meat or fish dishes. It is also often dried in thin slices and pan-fried for a crispy snack, similar to a potato chip.

Cherimoya

The cherimoya resembles a heart-shaped fruit that is about four to eight inches long and up to four inches wide, weighing on the average 5-1/2 to 18 ounces. Size is proportional to the number of seeds within. Remember to buy smaller if you don't like too many seeds.

The fruit tastes like a blend of pineapple, mango, and strawberry flavors and is very fragrant. Cherimoyas ripe within two to seven days when left at room temperature.

Coconut
The coconut is a fibrous fruit that grows year-round on tall palm trees, native to Asian countries such as India. When harvested, it has an outer husk that surrounds a hard shell with a seed inside. The coconut is famous for its sweet meat and milk that can be accessed after opening the outer layer. The riper the coconuts, the less milk; if you are looking for a coconut with a lot of milk, pick a green one.

Lychee Nuts
The lychee is typically strawberry-red, though it may have a pinkish or amber shade. Most lychees are oval, and 1 1/2 inches long. They have a thin, rough skin and are easily peeled when fresh. Inside, they are creamy and white, soft, and juicy.
The center of the lychee is fragrant and sweet and is best eaten fresh or when added to a fruit salad.

Mango
Mangos are a large oval smooth-skinned fruit with a juicy fragrant pulp and a large hairy seed. Mangos are great for a snack or for juice, preserves, or flavoring for ice cream. When buying a mango, make sure that they are firm and fragrant. Avoid mangos that have bruises or soft spots.

Papaya
An orange-fleshed, melon-like fruit, the papaya ripens at room temperature. Buy them when firm and eat them when soft and yellow in color.
Papaya is sweet and often enjoyed in ice creams, salads, preserves, juices, or simply alone with a wedge of lime or sugar. Unripe papaya is commonly used for cooking.

Pineapple
With a sweet flavor and unique pinecone shape and texture, pineapple is often a favorite ingredient in many desserts and drinks. They make a superb addition to yogurt, fruit salads, juices, baked sweets, and preserves.

Look for a soft, orange complexion, and avoid all others when possible. Pull on the top leaves; they should fall off easily with a quick tug. Smell the bottom of the fruit; its sweet fragrance should be easily noticeable.

Plantain
Similar to a banana, plantains are green when unripe, turning yellow, and then black when fully ripened. Hard and starchy, they must be cooked before eaten, whether ripe or unripe. Their flavor is often compared to potatoes but ripe plantains can be agreeably sweet.

Passion Fruit
This oval-shaped, lime-size fruit has bright orange, highly perfumed tart flesh. The skin can be red, brown, purple, or green.
The flesh is full of tiny black seeds that are edible, although not to everyone's delight. The pulp is strained and commonly enjoyed in juice form. Passion fruit is excellent in sauces and cocktails.

Star Fruit
Star fruit is a lengthened, yellow, deeply corrugated fruit that forms a five-pointed star when sliced crosswise.
The juicy, crispy flesh combines the acidity of citrus with the sweetness of grape. It is often eaten raw in a salad or, when fully ripe, enjoyed as a dessert.

Sapodilla
The fleshy, brown-colored fruit is the size of a small tomato and has a thin, darkish-brown skin and off-white interior.
The sapodilla has the tang and texture of cinnamon, apple, and pear combined together. The fruit is acerbic when unripe and must be fully ripened and soft before consumed.

Sugar Apple
The sugar apple has a thick crusty rind and black seeds. The interior is white and is sweet. It has a flavor similar to that of custard. Enjoy the sugar apple by slicing off sections or remove the pulp and mash it to make juice.

Tamarind
The fruit is brown and fleshy with a tangy taste, very different from others. The tamarind's unique flavor makes it ideal for seasoning foods such as chutneys, curries, or pickled fish and is usually used in Asian cuisine.

Citrus
Low in calories and sodium, high in Vitamin C, citrus fruits were once rare, given as gifts on occasions. The many varieties are listed below.

Blood Orange: The orange rind hides its deep red flesh and has an addictive sweetness that hints of raspberry.

Clementine: Small, thin-skinned oranges that are easy to peel, with neat, separate sections, and few or no seeds, make it ideal for quick and easy snacking. Loaded with Vitamin C, they are a nice accompaniment for a tray of Spanish cheeses.

Key Lime: This small, yellow-green fruit is commonly squeezed over green salads, atop seafood soups and fish dishes, or added to rum drinks of all varieties. Key lime is an excellent source of Vitamin C.

Kumquat: This small fruit of the citrus family has a sweet, edible rind and a juicy, slightly bitter flesh. It makes a great addition to salads and can be used in preserves and jams.

Navel Orange: They are large, thick-skinned, seedless, very juicy and sweet. Ortanique: A favorite as juice, or when eaten fresh.

Pomelo: The largest of all citrus fruits, this pear-shaped fruit has an orange-yellow rind and can be eaten like a grapefruit.

Satsuma: This large, seedless mandarin native to Japan is thin-skinned and easy to peel. It is mildly flavored and has a light orange-green rind.

Tangelo: This citrus fruit is a cross between grapefruit and tangerines, with a distinctive tart taste that compliments other fruits. Its juice is apt for salad dressings and as sauces for meats.

Tangerine: This sweet citrus is short and has a bright orange rind. It can be easily peeled and sectioned. Remember to remove the bitter white membranes before consumption.

Unique Fruit: Its ugly, speckled skin disguises one of the natural juiciest and sweetest treats today. Great as a snack or a juice, they are much sought after.

Valencia: This citrus fruit is a thin-skinned orange of high juice content and few seeds.

Grapes
Today, most grapes end up as wine, raisins, and juice; however, they can also be found whole. Grapes are available in all varieties such as red and blue-black grapes, as well as other green and yellow varieties.

Since they are convenient and easier to eat, seedless varieties are preferred, although seeded varieties are said to have a more robust flavor. The fresh grape season begins in May and runs through the month of January, with imported varieties filling in the rest of the year. The ripening process stops after harvest, so don't worry about overripe fruits. Always select grapes that are firm, ripe, clean, and not too tightly packed on the stem. The grapes should be uniformly shaped and have a somewhat chalky color to them. Avoid grapes that are wrinkled, dully colored, or have limp stalks; all these are a clear indication of decay.

Tomatoes
Tomatoes contain lycopene, a powerful antioxidant that helps prevent prostate cancer. They are also beneficial for the heart. Their seeds, however, are indigestible and pass through the system. Tomatoes are excellent additives to food, as they have an acidic property that helps bring out the flavors of other foods. Culinary uses of tomatoes include pastes, ketchup, pizza sauce, tomato pie, and so on.

When buying tomatoes, make sure they are firm and avoid any with spots, shriveled skin, or bruises.

Melons
Melons are of many varieties, such as the summer and winter varieties, on a broader classification. Summer melons are fragrant, flavorful, and unfortunately quickly perishable. Peak season for melons is late spring to early summer, depending on the variety. Summer melons include both cantaloupes and muskmelons; don't get confused upon classification. The size and skin color of these fruits can vary widely, but the flesh is usually a pale orange.
The best way to judge the ripeness of a melon is to simply press on the end opposite to the stem; it should yield noticeably to the pressure of your finger. Summer melons are normally more fragrant than winter melons, but fragrance alone is not a sure indication of ripeness.

To buy melons, choose those that are heavy for their size and free of bruises or other damage. Check the navel, or stem end, for excessive softness and mold. Except for true cantaloupes that come with partial stem attached, summer melons should not have an attached stem.

Pears
Pears come in two distinctive types: European and Asian. Although they have a vaguely parallel taste, they are different. European pears are matured off the tree while Asian pears are left on the tree until ripe. Asian pears are shaped more like apples, while European ones have an oval pear shape. European pears have a soft, smooth texture while Asian pears are crisp. Regardless, pears are a seasonal treasure.

One medium pear has about 100 calories and is a good source of fiber, particularly if eaten unpeeled. They also contain significant amounts of Vitamin C and potassium.

Asian Pears
Best eaten cold and crisp, keep them refrigerated and humidified in a loosely closed bag. Most varieties will stay as long as three months, however, they tend to acquire a wine-like flavor if kept too long. The flesh of Asian pears does not brown as quickly as that of European ones. Some develop discoloration, but this is largely caused by excessive sugar, not oxidation.

European Pears
European pears ripen at room temperature. Keep them in a fruit bowl and check for maturity by pressing gently near the stem. If the flesh yields, the pear should be consumed immediately as it is a sure indicator of ripeness.
Like Asian pears, ripening of European pears can be delayed by refrigerating and humidifying. When ripe, consume immediately or refrigerate for a few days. Lengthy refrigeration when fully ripe will make them mealy and are excellent in sauces and smoothies or as a thickening agent in stews and soups.

Stone Fruits
Most fruits of summer are known as stone fruits because of the stone-like pit at the core such as peaches, plums, cherries, and apricots. When fully ripe and at the peak of their season, the simplest way to enjoy stone fruits is to eat them fresh.

Apricots
When ripe, apricots offer a sweet and tangy lusciousness that surpasses other fruits. Although not as popular as peaches, apricots create lifelong fans.
Apricots are the first of the fruits to appear in summer. When choosing fresh apricots, look for orange-colored fruits, although some will have a reddish cheek. Even when partially unripe, apricots should yield to gentle pressure and exude a sweet fragrance; the skin should be smooth and velvety in texture.

Cherries
To choose cherries, look for plump, firm fruits with their stems intact. Buy cherries that have been kept cool and moist, as flavor and texture both suffer at warm temperatures. Take just a few cherries at a time in your hand and select only the best. Good cherries should be large, glossy, plump, hard, and dark colored for their variety. The stems should always be fresh and green, a sign of freshness. Check carefully for bruises or cuts on the surface, and put back cherries that are sticky as a result of juice leakage.

Nectarines
Nectarines are perfect for delicious pies, cobblers, or fresh fruit salads. Choose brightly colored nectarines that yield to gentle pressure, especially

along the seam. Firm or moderately hard fruits will ripen quickly if kept at room temperature in a loosely closed paper bag away from sunlight. A rosy color is not an indication of ripeness, so don't be tempted. Avoid hard or greenish nectarines as well as those that are too soft or shriveled.

Peaches
When buying peaches, find one with skin that shows a background color of yellow—the amount of pink or red blush depends on the variety and is not a reliable sign of ripeness. Slight hints of green indicate the peaches were picked too soon and will not ripen properly. Look for plump, medium- to large-sized peaches with smooth firm skins. Choose fruits that are mildly, not strongly, fragrant.

Also, try to avoid extremely hard peaches and choose those that yield slightly to pressure along the "seam". Peaches at this stage of ripeness will soften well when kept at room temperature for a few days in a paper bag.

Avoid dark-colored, mushy, bruised peaches that are a clear indication of being overripe. Tan circles or spots on the skin are also some clear early signs of decay.

Plums
Plums should be plump and well colored. If the fruit yields to gentle pressure, it is ready for consumption; however, you can buy plums that are fairly firm and let them soften at home. Ripe plums will be slightly soft at the stem and tip; avoid those with shriveled skin, mushy spots, or breaks in the skin, a sure indication of decay.

Vegetables
*Vegetable Nutrition Facts

Key Nutrients

Veggie	Calories	Carb. gm.	Fiber gm.	Protein gm.	Potassium mg.	Sodium mg.	Vit A	Vit C	Calcium	Iron
							\% Daily Value			
Artichokes, 1 med. raw	60	13	7	4	470	120	4	25	6	10
Asparagus, 5 spears, raw	25	4	2	2	230	0	10	15	2	2
Beets, 1 med. raw	35	8	2	1	270	65	*	6	*	4

Bell Pepper (Green) 1 med, raw	30	8	2	1	210	0	15	180	*	4
Bell Pepper (Red) 1 med, raw	30	8	2	1	210	0	140	380	*	4
Black Radish, 50 g. raw	10	2	< 1	< 1	n/a	10	*	20	*	*
Bok Choy, 1/2 head, raw	50	9	4	6	1060	270	250	320	45	20
Broccoli, 3 med. spears, raw	25	5	3	3	300	25	30	140	4	4
Brussels Sprouts, 5 med. raw	40	9	4	3	370	25	15	130	4	8
Burdock, 1 med. raw	110	27	5	2	480	10	*	8	6	6
Cabbage (Green), 200 g. raw	60	12	5	2	450	50	*	170	10	4
Cabbage (Red), 200 g. raw	50	12	4	3	410	20	*	190	10	6
Carrots, 1 med, raw	35	8	2	1	280	40	270	10	2	0
Cauliflower, 1/4 med. head	35	7	3	3	400	45	*	150	2	2
Celery, 1 med. stalk, raw	10	3	1	< 1	180	50	*	8	2	*
Celery Root, 100 g. raw	40	9	2	2	300	100	*	15	4	4
Cilantro, 50 g. raw	10	2	1	1	260	25	60	30	4	4
Collard Greens, 100 g. chopped, raw	30	6	4	2	170	20	80	60	15	*
Corn, Sweet, 1 large ear, raw	120	27	4	5	390	20	8	15	*	4
Cucumber, 1 med, raw	45	9	3	3	520	0	10	30	6	6
Daikon Radish, 50 g. raw	10	2	< 1	< 1	115	10	*	20	*	*
Eggplant, 1 med unpeeled, raw	140	33	14	6	1190	15	10	15	4	8
Endive	10	2	2	< 1	110	0	*	2	*	*
Fava, 1 cup fresh (not dried)	80	13	5	6	270	55	8	60	2	10

Fennel, 1 med. bulb, raw	70	17	7	3	970	120	6	45	10	10
Garlic, 2 cloves, raw	10	2	<1	<1	2	0	*	4	*	*
Ginger, 25 g. raw, sliced	15	4	<1	<1	105	0	*	2	*	*
Green Beans, 100 g. raw	30	6	4	1	240	0	4	10	4	2
Horseradish Root, 1 TB fresh	10	2	<1	<1	85	0	*	30	*	*
Jerusalem Artichoke, 100 g. raw	80	17	2	2	430	0	*	6	*	20
Jicama, 1 small, raw	140	32	18	3	550	15	*	120	4	10
Kale, 100 g. raw	50	10	2	3	450	45	180	200	15	10
Kohlrabi, 100 g. raw	25	6	4	2	350	20	*	100	2	2
Leeks, 1 med. raw	50	13	2	1	160	20	*	20	6	10
Lettuce (Boston, Bibb, Butter) 1 head	20	4	2	2	420	10	30	20	6	2
Lettuce (Iceberg) 1/2 head	45	9	3	3	350	30	10	20	6	6
Lettuce, Red or Green Leaf, 100 g.	20	4	2	1	260	10	40	30	6	8
Lettuce (Romaine) 100 g. inner leaf	15	2	2	2	290	10	50	40	4	6
Mushrooms (Crimini), 50 g. raw	10	2	0	1	220	0	*	*	*	*
Mushrooms (Enoki), 10 med. raw	10	2	<1	<1	115	0	*	6	*	*
Mushrooms (Shiitake), 100 g. raw	25	5	1	2	n/a	0	*	4	*	8
Mustard Greens, 100 g. raw	25	5	3	3	350	25	110	120	10	8
Okra, 100 g. raw	35	8	3	2	300	10	15	35	8	4
Onion (Pearl), 100 g. raw	40	9	2	1	160	0	*	10	2	*
Onion (Red), 1 med, raw	40	9	2	1	170	0	*	10	2	*

Onion (Yellow), 1 med, raw	40	9	2	1	170	0	*	10	2	*
Parsley, 1 cup fresh, chopped	20	4	2	2	330	35	60	130	8	20
Parsnip, 100 g. raw	80	18	5	1	380	10	*	30	4	4
Potato, 1 med. raw	100	26	3	4	720	0	*	45	2	6
Pumpkin, 1 cup boiled, mashed	50	12	3	2	560	0	50	20	4	8
Radish, 3 each	5	1	n/a	< 1	100	10	*	15	*	*
Rhubarb, 1 cup raw, diced	25	6	2	1	350	0	2	15	10	*
Rutabaga, 1 small, raw	70	16	5	2	650	40	20	80	10	6
Salsify, 100 g. raw	80	19	3	3	380	20	*	15	6	4
Savoy Cabbage, 1 cup raw, shredded	20	4	2	1	160	20	15	35	2	*
Scallion, 100 g. raw	30	7	3	2	280	15	8	30	8	8
Snow Peas, 100 g. raw	40	8	3	3	200	0	2	100	4	10
Spinach, 100 g. raw	20	4	3	3	560	80	130	45	10	15
Squash (Acorn), 1 raw	170	45	6	3	1500	15	30	80	15	15
Squash (Butternut), 1 cup cubed, raw	60	16	5	1	490	5	220	50	6	6
Squash (Crookneck), 100 g. raw	20	4	2	< 1	210	0	6	15	2	2
Squash (Hubbard), 100 g. raw	40	9	3	2	320	5	110	20	*	2
Sweet Potato, 1 med. raw	130	33	4	2	350	45	440	30	2	2
Swiss Chard, 100 g. raw	20	4	2	2	380	210	70	50	6	10
Taro Root	20	4	2	2	380	210	70	50	6	10
Tomato, med. raw **	35	7	1	1	360	5	20	40	2	2

Tomato (Cherry), 5 each, raw**	20	4	< 1	< 1	190	10	10	15	*	2
Tomato (Roma), 3 med. raw**	40	9	2	2	410	15	25	60	*	4
Turnip, 1 med, raw	35	8	2	1	230	80	*	45	4	2
Turnip Greens, 100 g. raw	25	6	3	2	300	40	150	100	20	6
Watercress, 1 cup raw, chopped	5	< 1	< 1	< 1	110	15	30	25	4	*
Yellow Wax Beans, 100 g. raw	30	7	3	2	210	5	2	25	4	6
Zucchini, 1 large raw	45	9	4	4	800	10	20	50	4	8

Amounts given are approximations; nutritional content will vary slightly, depending on growing conditions, etc.

Artichokes

Artichokes are commonly knows as lobsters of the vegetable world since it requires your hands to get to the delicious parts and both have conventionally been served with butter! For dipping, try roasted red pepper purée, a silken tofu-based garlic aioli, or add the hearts to pasta with feta cheese, fresh basil, and tomatoes.

Asparagus

Asparagus has been valued for its subtle flavor and texture. A member of the lily family, asparagus is a good source of Vitamin C and supplies folate, beta-carotene, and glutathione, an antioxidant.
They come in green, white, and purple varieties. When tender, lightly steamed asparagus goes extremely well with high-quality olive oil and fresh lemon juice. For oven-roasted asparagus, drizzle olive oil and splash balsamic vinegar.

Broccoli & Cauliflower

Broccoli and cauliflower are a variation of cabbage in which the flowering phase of the plant is halted in advance. They are famous for their wealth of valuable phytochemicals that sustain health through removal of free radicals in the body.

Broccoli

One of the most popular spring vegetables, broccoli is commonly cooked with olive oil, white wine, and freshly minced garlic.
Broccoli consists of two general types: sprouting broccoli, which is spring

harvested, and calabrese, which is summer harvested. Broccoli is best harvested when young and tender; look for stalks that are slender and crisp. The florets should be tight and darkly colored, a sign of freshness. Yellowish florets are a suggestion of age; pale green florets specify a lack of valuable phytochemicals.

Cauliflower
Cauliflower curds are white, lacking the chlorophyll that lends green color to other cruciferous vegetables. Harvest crest transpire in the spring, summer, and fall depending on variety and climate.

Cauliflower should have condensed curds that are clean, uniformly white or creamy white, and firm to touch. Avoid cauliflowers that are bruised or spotted.

Brussels sprouts
Properly cooked, fresh Brussels sprouts have a subtle, slightly sweet and nutty flavor. Brussels sprouts are related to the broccoli and cabbage family. Like other brassicas, they are valuable for their content of vitamins C and A, folic acid, potassium, fiber, and protein.

Brussels sprouts are available year-round but are most abundant in autumn months through early spring months. Choose firm, small sprouts with good green color and stem ends that are clean and white.

The outer leaves contain the most nutrients, which emphasize the importance of avoiding any with wilted or yellowed leaves.

Cilantro
Cilantro looks like parsley, but it is extremely different in taste. Its bright citrus-like flavor adds an interesting tang to a wide range of foods, such as condiments and dips, stews, casseroles, soups, and sauces. Cilantro is a fragile herb; the leaves do not dry well and should always be used fresh and raw and always added at the last minute since cooking quickly depletes its flavor.

Coriander is not a substitute for cilantro, as the flavor and texture are not the same. The seeds are dried and can be kept for up to six months without a noticeable loss of quality. To appreciate its full flavor, toast gently just before use.

Cucumbers
They are split into two basic types: pickling and slicing.
Pickling varieties are smaller than slicing cucumbers, with thicker, bulgy skins,

and are usually harder to find. Salad cucumbers are available at all markets all year-round. Greenhouse cucumbers—sometimes called English cucumbers—are gaining in popularity because they are seedless and therefore easier to digest. Select firm cucumbers without damage that are heavy and rounded at the tips. Avoid any cucumbers that have shriveled tips or soft spots. They should have a rich green color, not yellow, and should be cool to the touch.

Fennel
Bitter Fennel
Bitter fennel is quite related to celery seed, having a somewhat bitter flavor, but the entire plant is edible, with the stalks often sliced and used in stews and pickles.

Sweet Fennel
Sweet fennel, like its bitter cousin, is entirely edible and is used primarily as a flavoring but also as a vegetable.

Florence fennel
Florence fennel, also known as finocchio, produces a swelling of overlapping stalks at its base that is used as a vegetable. Florence fennel can be sliced and fried or steamed, depending on how you prefer it, but is commonly used raw, sliced thinly and added into salads.

While the entire plants of both bitter and sweet fennel are edible, they are grown for their seed and are rarely available as vegetables.

Look for Florence fennel bulbs that are hard and clean. Bulbs are typically available with stalks and feathery leaves together. Fennel bulbs are sometimes sold with the stalks already cut off, a possible suggestion that they are not fresh. Avoid fennels if the cuts are dried and white and if there are splits or brown spots.

Fresh Beans
Beans eaten fresh are of two types: edible-pods that include green, snap, yellow wax, and scarlet runner, and shell beans that include fava, soybeans, and lima.

Edible-pod beans should be displayed open—not in bags—so you can pick out beans of equal size for uniform cooking. Choose beans that are free of spots and scars. They should have a vivid color and velvety feel, be straight and slender with a firm texture, and should snap when broken. Avoid beans that are stiff or if the seeds are greatly visible through the pod. Fresh beans should be firm and bulge should be noticeable through a tightly closed pod.

If already shelled, the beans should be plump and tight-skinned, a sign of freshness.

Garlic
Garlic is a very common vegetable and is available year-round. Look for bulbs that are fleshy and dense with numerous layers of dry flimsy husk. A heavy, firm bulb denotes that the garlic will be fresh, whereas a bulb that is light is probably old. Avoid damp or soft bulbs or those that have begun to sprout, as well as any that have dark, powdery patches under the skin.

Elephant garlic, though tempting because of its size, is not true garlic but more closely related to the leek. It does not have the same health benefits as regular garlic nor does it match its flavor.

Leafy Greens
From kale to green spinach, leafy greens are overflowing with nutrition, flavor, and versatility.

Fresh, tasty leafy greens are available year-round, but they do have their peak seasons. Collards, kale, turnip greens, and mustard greens are at their best from the month of October. Swiss chard and beet greens are best from the spring through fall. Dandelion greens are best in the spring and summer.
When buying, look for crisp leaves with a fresh green color. Stems should appear freshly cut, the leaves should be crisp, and the color should be extremely vibrant, sure indicators of freshness. Yellowing is definitely a sign of age and should be avoided.

Leeks
They are related to the onion family but are milder and sweeter with a crisp texture when cooked. Leeks are more nourishing than onions, containing more vitamins and minerals.

When buying leeks, choose those that are firm and slender with clean white necks. The necks should be straight and stiff all the way to the root end. Tops should be fresh and green. If the stalk itself is limp, it is an indication of age.

Mushrooms
Cremini, button, and Portobello mushrooms are actually closely related. Cremini looks and tastes much like a button mushroom but is larger with a brown cap. When development is unchecked, it becomes a Portobello with complex flavoring and texture.
Other types of mushrooms found in the market are:

Chanterelle
Curved vase shaped with color varying from bright orange to apricot gold. To enjoy the flavor, simply sautée with olive oil.

Enoki
Tiny mushrooms, with creamy white cap on a long slender stem. They are best raw in salads, floating on soups, or stir-fried just before serving.

Morel
Tan to dark brown in color with spongy caps that hide a hollow interior these mushrooms must be rinsed before cooking. These mushrooms complement meat dishes well. Fresh morels sautéed in butter are delicious on their own. They are available fresh in spring and dried year-round.

In general, shrunken, slippery, or bruised mushrooms should be avoided. Unless they are actually spoiled, older mushrooms are not necessarily a bad choice. For cooking, choose smaller mushrooms, whereas for slicing or chopping, medium-sized varieties are better. For stuffing, choose mushrooms with large caps, as it is easier.

Okra
Okra is a good source of Vitamin C, lutein, magnesium, and potassium, among others. It is also high in dietary fiber and excellent for the body. Small, young pods—no more than 3" long—are your best bet. Choose okra pods that are clean, fresh, and green, a clear sign of freshness. They should snap crisply when broken in half. Avoid pods that look dull and dry, as okra becomes fibrous and tough when over-matured and thus are difficult to eat.

Onions
Onions are a rich source of phytochemicals that promote healthy blood pressure and cholesterol levels, making them a valuable addition to a healthy diet. Onions are divided into two categories: sweet and storage.

Sweet Onions
Sweet onions are fresher, sweeter, and milder because of being harvested in the spring and early summer. They do not keep as well as storage onions. The sweetness is due to a combination of high sugar levels and low sulfur content.

Whether you are shopping for sweet or storage onions, choose ones that are dry and solid with no soft spots or sprouts. The skin should be dry, shiny, and tight around the neck.

Large onions are best for salads, sandwiches, and a better choice for peeling or chopping. Small to medium onions are best for recipes such as stews that require less cutting and peeling.

Onion Relatives

Boiling or Pearl Onions
These are simply undeveloped onions useful for kebabs, stews, or pickling.

Chives
A dark-green plant with hollow stems that produces purple or pink globe-shaped blossoms in mid-summer. Their deep color and mild flavor make them valuable in dips and spreads.
The blossoms are edible and are used as a garnish. Chives lend a subtle aromatic taste to eggs, chicken, or fish.

Cippolini Onions
Cippolini onions are a small to medium yellow onion with a flattened saucer shape and thin skins.

Leeks
A mild and refined member of the onion family, leeks have long been favored in many cuisines.

Scallions and Green onions
Scallions and green onions are immature onions. More perishable than regular onions, they are also highly nutritious. The green tops have more Vitamin C, folate, calcium, and beta-carotene than regular onions and, therefore, present a better healthy and nutritious option.

Shallots
Shallots are the stylish onions, long associated with French haute cuisine. They have a delicate flavor that is suggestive of both onions and garlic. Shallots grow in clusters of small bulbs that are attached at the base with skins that are thin and copper-red in color.

Peas
Several varieties of peas are found in the market such as sugar snap peas, with an edible pod perfect for snacking; garden peas, when shelled, are wonderful steamed or in soups, salads, and grain dishes; and snow peas, an essential ingredient in stir-fries. Peas are an excellent source of folate, Vitamin A and Vitamin C, and a good source of zinc, an essential healthy vegetable.

Pumpkins
Pumpkins are a fruit, closely related to cucumbers, watermelon, and other squash. They are used in many ways such as processing dried pieces into flour, drying and roasting the seeds, eating the blossoms and weaving strips that are pounded flat, and dried into durable mats.

Pumpkins can be diced and steamed as a side vegetable; mixed with fruits, such as apples, pears, or rhubarb; and used in potpies, soufflés, salads, and soups.

For cooking, avoid the large jack-o'-lantern varieties—the best cooking varieties are small but heavy for their size. Make sure they have at least an inch of stem and no blemishes or soft spots.

Root Vegetables
Root vegetables are incredibly and available best from October to March. In general, root vegetables are low in calories with virtually no fat.

Asian Turnip
Asian turnips look like over-sized carrots with a grayish white color. Choose a turnip that is short with a firm, smooth surface—always a safe bet.

Beet
Beets are valued for their sweetness but are very low in calories. Fresh beets have twice the folic acid and potassium and a distinctive flavor not found in canned beets. Choose firm round roots, with deep-red flesh and green leaves with either green or red veins. Beets are good roasted, steamed, and braised in soups or salads.

Burdock
Burdock is a carrot-like vegetable with brown skin and white flesh. Cooking removes any bitterness that might be in the vegetable. Look for firm roots and scrub well before consumption. You can use burdocks in broths or stir-fries.

Carrot
Carrots as a rule should be firm, smooth-skinned, without cracks or small rootlets. Look for red- or purple-colored varieties, known for their anthocyanin content.

Celeriac or Celery Root
Celeriac is grown for its round root that has a celery-like flavor. It is about 4 inches in diameter with a light brown, bulb-type root. It can be used in soups,

stews, or purées.
A number of other root vegetables are also available in the market.

Spring Onions and Spring Garlic
With similar nutritional benefits as spring garlic, these can be chopped and added raw to soups or salads. Spring onions contain quercetin, like other onions, and have a mild flavor.

Spring Salad Mix
The mixtures vary widely with a balance between mild, slightly bitter, and peppery flavors and contain some or all of the following: Arugula, Dandelion, Frisée, Lettuce, Mizuna, Purslane, Red Mustard, Swiss Chard, Tat Soi, and Watercress.

Salad mixes are sold in bulk or bags; always check for slimy or yellowed liquid and wilting leaves. Bright colors and a crisp look are a suggestion of freshness.

Sweet Corn
Sweet corn can be yellow, white, or a combination of both, commonly called bicolor. Look for husks that are fresh, tight, and green—a clear indication of freshness. Peel back part of the husk to see if the ears are well filled with milky kernels. Excessively large or depressed kernels are a sign of over-maturity. The silk should be moist, soft, and light gold—another very sure sign of fresh corn.

Winter Squash
Winter squash is also commonly known as hard squash, and is available in a variety of shapes, colors, and sizes.

Acorn
Acorn is a small, deep-green or pumpkin-colored squash. Excellent when baked and drizzled with butter, maple syrup, and a pinch of cinnamon—an easy snack.

Blue Hubbard
These are typically large with a unique, beautiful color. A lovely centerpiece when filled with stuffing—sure to catch ample attention and appreciation.

Buttercup
They are round and green with grey coloring. Firm, delicious, and perfect for a fruity stuffing or chunks in soup.

Butternut
A bell-shaped tan-colored squash with sweet orange flesh. They are delicious when cubed and added to stews with warm-flavored seasonings such as cloves, cardamom, curry, cayenne, and paprika.

Above, are only a few of the delicious varieties found in the market.

CHAPTER 14

LET'S GO SHOPPING:
Everything you need to get started now!

You can start stocking up on nutritious foods to help you reduce your risk of heart disease, diabetes, and other diseases. There is no need to go out and buy everything on the list; these are suggestions to get you started. Fresh organic fruits and vegetables:

- Fresh seasonal fruits—These include berries, oranges, apples, pears, bananas, mangoes, and grapes.

- Dried fruits—Some of these are raisins, dried cranberries, dates, and dried apricots. These are great as snacks when soaked and can be tossed in salads, baked goods and even a main course.

- Fresh seasonal vegetables—Among these choices are yellow, green, and red bell peppers; cucumbers; broccoli; kale; escarole; cauliflower; tomatoes; dark leafy greens; celery; eggplant; zucchini; yellow squash; acorn squash; spaghetti squash; and many others.

Dairy and dairy alternatives:
Lactose is milk sugar and occurs naturally in the milk of animals. Many people are sensitive to milk products because they lack the enzyme called lactase. This enzyme, found in the gastrointestinal tract, is critical in the digestion of lactose. If the lactase enzyme is missing or depleted, the gastrointestinal tract can not adequately break down the milk sugar, leading to a wide variety of symptoms. When this occurs, these individuals are described as being "lactose intolerant".

Symptoms from lactose intolerance can vary greatly from one individual to the next as well as vary within the individual. These symptoms include but are not limited to:

- stomach cramps
- intestinal bloating or "pot belly"
- flatulence
- diarrhea
- headaches
- nausea

Organic milk from pasture-fed cows (Raw milk has been known to cure many of the above digestive conditions because it naturally contains healthy bacteria that inhibit the growth of undesirable and dangerous organisms. Without these friendly bacteria, pasteurized milk is more susceptible to contamination.)

- Coconut milk
- Nut or rice milk
- Organic buttermilk
- Organic goat cheese
- Organic yogurt or kefir
- Organic sour cream
- Free range organic brown eggs

Fats, cooking oils

Researchers are starting to realize that low-fat diets are not a cure-all for disease prevention and weight loss. A significant study published in the Journal of the American Medical Association in early 2006 found that women eating a low-fat diet had the same rates of heart disease and cancer as those who had no dietary fat restrictions after eight years. The evidence seems to indicate that, instead of controlling or cutting fat, it is smarter to eat the right kinds of fat—primarily monounsaturated fats, along with adequate amounts of omega-3 fatty acids from fish and fish oils—while at the same time eliminating harmful hydrogenated fats and highly processed vegetable oils from your diet. As part of a balanced and varied diet, use a variety of oils, including oils from different sources and oils that contain different kinds of fatty acids. Do not use a single oil to the exclusion of all others—any food in excess is not recommended.

- Assorted raw nuts and seeds
- Ghee (organic kosher butter can be kept at room temperature)
- Whole or ground flaxseeds
- Olive oil
- Avocado Oil
- Canola Oil
- Coconut Oil
- Corn Oil
- Grapeseed Oil
- Olive Oil
- Palm Oil
- Peanut Oil
- Safflower Oil-High Oleic
- Sesame Oil
- Sunflower Oil-High Oleic
- Walnut Oil
- Flax Oil

Herbs, seasonings and spices:
Remember the radiation of normal store seasonings. Look for the organic alternatives:

- All of the herbs mentioned in the previous chapter plus:

- Celtic salt or sea salt, bay leaves, black pepper, caraway seeds, cayenne and chili powder, and garlic powder

- Chinese five-spice, cinnamon, cloves, coriander, cumin, and curry powder, and all-spice

- Dill, garlic powder, ground ginger, Italian seasoning, and marjoram

- Nutmeg, onion powder, oregano, paprika, and parsley

- Red pepper flakes, rosemary, and Bragg's Liquid Aminos (a healthier fermented soy alternative loaded with flavor)

Sweeteners:
- Stevia (liquid or powder form)

- Organic grade A maple syrups

- Raw honey (bee pollen included)

- Turbinado or raw cane sugar

- Agave (comes from a cactus plant) as a sweet alternative to use when baking and even tastes great in lemonade. Agave is an excellent sugar substitute for diabetics, as it ranks low on the Glycemic Index.

Pantry essentials:
- Assorted dried beans
- Reduced-sodium soup mixes with dry beans
- Rolled, steel cut, or Irish oats
- Oat bran
- Organic whole wheat pastry flour
- Buckwheat flour
- Whole-grain cold cereals
- Barley
- Brown rice, wild rice, and/or brown basmati rice
- Grains such as wheat berries and whole wheat, spelt, or kamut pastas

- baking potatoes, red potatoes, and sweet potatoes
- Whole grain breads, tortillas, or pitas
- Whole grain, trans-fat free organic table crackers
- Flax meal
- Buckwheat flour and whole-wheat pastry flour
- Non GMO organic cornmeal
- Organic tomato paste
- Organic pasta sauce in jar
- Reduced sodium organic chicken, beef, or vegetable broths
- Assorted vinegars: rice, red wine, balsamic, or apple cider

Frozen foods:
- Frozen vegetables and vegetable blends without added sauces, gravies, and added sodium

- Frozen fruits without added sugar

- Free range organic meat, poultry, and deep ocean fish

- Free range organic skinless, boneless chicken or turkey breasts and tenders

- Organic, skinless, white breast meat ground chicken or turkey

- Organic, lean ground beef such as ground round or ground sirloin that comes from organic, Pasteur fed cows

- Assorted fish: salmon, mackerel, tilapia, trout, herring, and tuna

- Tempeh

- Seitan

Stocking your cupboard with these heart-healthy items will encourage you and your family members to eat more heart-healthfully. Having these items on-hand will also make menu and meal preparation a snap and prepare you for the quick, delicious recipes available to you in the following chapters.

CHAPTER 15

THE WELLNESS KITCHEN
Cooking for Health and Weightloss

COOKING MEATS

The way you cook and prepare the foods you eat can either add or subtract nutritional value. You can fry an organic chicken in a tub of lard and negate all the good reasons for going organic by adding to your already high cholesterol level. Or you can decide to roast it and make gravy out of the juices from the roasting pot instead.

Stir-fry has been popular for centuries in Asia and has become very popular in the United States for health food lovers. It is a low-fat and tasty way to cook your meat and you do not need a wok to do it. You can use a sturdy pan that can sizzle, although a wok can retain the flavors and juices of your meat much more efficiently.

Be sure to use very high heat that sears and smokes the food. Cut the meat, poultry, or fish into bite-size pieces for better results. With stir-fry, the vegetables are the main dish; meats are only for seasoning. Go heavy on the vegetables and lighter on the meat. Avoid crowding the food in the pan; it may steam instead of sizzle.

Roasting and cooking in palm leaves (an old Thai cooking method) is an excellent idea since you don't expose your food to the aluminum that comes from traditional foil. Palm leaves keep your food nice and tender and loaded with flavor. Food steams in its natural juices and the flavors are more concentrated. I said it was tasty, but you don't want to make gravy out of the juices left over.

Try wine. Marinate your meats or make sauces out of the wine. When wine burns off during the cooking process, it also burns off calories. Wine is great for the heart, and it also is an amazing antioxidant loaded with natural bioflavonoid.

If you like your chicken fried, you don't have to give it up completely. Try frying your chicken in the oven. Oven frying is usually recommended to patients to reduce cholesterol levels. It actually has a better flavor coming from the oven than a tub of grease on the stove.

COOKING AND/OR PREPARING VEGETABLES

Vegetables are an essential part of our lives, and they have their own benefits. In order to maximize these benefits, we need to learn the efficient method by which to prepare and eat them. Cooked vegetables lose vitamins, minerals, colors, and flavors when not cooked properly. Some efficient healthy ways to prepare vegetables are as follows:

Steaming
Steaming is quick, preserves nutrients, and works best for fresh or frozen vegetables such as carrots, broccoli, spinach, peas, and beans. If you don't have a steaming basket, you can fill a pot with mixed vegetables and add some unsalted water and steam. Don't forget to keep the remaining broth, as it makes excellent soup.

Roasting
Roasting is quick, effortless, and a superb method for cooking vegetables, as it preserves the vitamins, flavors, and minerals. In a large bowl, cover sliced vegetables with olive oil; add garlic powder, onion powder, salt and pepper to taste. Place them on a cookie sheet and roast at 350° until tender.

Stir-Fry
Stir-frying is another very good flavor- and color-preserving cooking method for vegetables. Sliced vegetables are put in a frying pan covered at bottom with any liquid such as water or broth. Stir the vegetables constantly and vigorously until they are crispy and glossy.

Panning
Vegetables can also be cooked by steam produced by their own vegetable juices. In a frying pan, add a little olive oil, sliced vegetables, and your favorite seasonings. Cover the pan, put it on medium heat, and within 5-8 minutes your vegetables will be ready. Panning is an efficient way of preparing carrots, beans, and shredded cabbage.

Raw
One of the best ways to retain all of the enzymes and nutrients in your vegetables is by eating it raw. When preparing your produce, you can enhance the flavor by adding freshly made sauces and herbs to your dish. Your vegetables can be tossed in the sauce or blended through a food processor or Vitamix juicer to make raw soup or salsa.

THE RIGHT KINDS OF FAT

The AHA suggests a daily fat ingestion limited to 30% of your day's total calories. The studies also highlight that the type of fat you eat may be just as important as the amount. People who eat a diet high in monounsaturated fat were found to have a lower risk of heart disease than those who eat extra saturated fats.

Here are a few examples of healthy and unhealthy fats:

Healthy fats	Unhealthy fats	In The Middle
Peanut butter	Marbled meats	Chicken
Olive oil	Organ meats	Fish
Avocados	Butter	Lean red meat
Soybeans	Ice cream	
Nuts	Mayonnaise	
Canola oil	Milk	
Corn oil	Cream	
Sesame, sunflower and pumpkin seeds	Cheese	
	Palm oil	
Grapeseed vegenaise mayo alternative	Any food made with hydrogenated oils	

PORTIONS

Healthy eating plans call for a certain amount of servings of fruits, vegetables, carbohydrates, and such. However, exactly how much is a serving of broccoli or a serving of meat? Estimating serving sizes is easier than you think. All you have to do it find a convenient reference such as the ones explained below.

The Comparison Method

One way to determine how much you're eating is to compare a serving size with a familiar object, something you are less likely to forget. A few common comparisons include, equating one ounce of cheese to a pair of dice, three ounces of meat to a deck of cards, one serving of fruit to a baseball, one serving of bread to a cassette tape and so on.

The Pre-Measured Method

Another method is to pre-measure all food portions. Buy a good set of measuring spoons, a glass measuring cup for liquids, a set of measuring cups for dry foods, and a kitchen scale for weighing other food groups such as meat or cheese. In addition, a smart trick is to use a smaller plate as it encourages smaller portions.

Weigh raw fruits and vegetables, but weigh meat, poultry, and fish only after cooking. Recommended serving size for meat and such is three ounces.

The Hand Method

Some people use their hands to estimate portion size. These measurements are for an average-sized woman's hand such as thumb volume equals one ounce, fist volume equals one cup of paste or cooked vegetables, the palm area equals one serving of fish or meat, and two handfuls will equal one serving of snack foods.

FIVE SMALL MEALS

Whether you are trying to lose weight, gain weight, or just planning to eat healthy, 5 or 6 small meals a day is more beneficial than conventional three big meals. This statement is logical for many reasons such as: the body is only proficient at utilizing a limited number of nutrients at a time. With small meals, there is better opportunity for nutrient absorption, therefore leading to healthier eating. The six meals a day diet plan is also thought to be effective at greatly reducing cholesterol levels. In addition, the body is more likely to store fat when it is unsure of when it will get its next feeding. Your body is extremely smart and whether or not you plan, it does. When it becomes used to being fed constantly to six meals a day, it tends not to worry about the future and less likely to store unsightly fat.

FOOD COMBINING

Many people believe that the human stomach should be able to digest any number of different foods at the same time. However, digestion is governed by one's physiology and biochemistry. Ultimately, it is not what we eat that is crucial to our health but what we digest and assimilate. To assimilate means to take in and absorb. What can help this process of assimilation are digestive enzymes. Your body secretes digestive enzymes in very specific amounts and at very specific times. Certain foods require certain types of digestive enzyme secretions. For example, carbohydrate foods require carbohydrate-splitting enzymes (amylase), whereas protein foods require protein splitting enzymes (protease), etc. Improperly combining foods can cause poor assimilation of nutrients, which can lead to indigestion and a host of digestive disorders. It is with this understanding and a comprehensive knowledge of the digestive process that led many health practitioners to promote efficient food combing. The following represents a brief summary of the rules followed by easy to follow food combining charts:

- Carbohydrate foods and acid foods should not be eaten at the same meal. In other words, avoid eating your starches with fruit. For example, do not eat bread, rice, or potatoes with lemons, limes, oranges, grapefruits, pineapples, tomatoes, or other sour fruits. This is because the enzyme, ptyalin, acts only in an alkaline environment and can easily be destroyed by even the smallest amount of acid! Fruit acids not only prevent your body from digesting carbohydrate, but they also cause fermentation.

- Do not eat a concentrated protein and a concentrated carbohydrate at the same meal. This means do not eat nuts, meat, eggs, cheese, or other protein foods at the same meal with bread, cereals, potatoes, sweet fruits, cakes, etc. Candy and sugar greatly reduces the secretion of gastric juice and can upset stomach activity if consumed in large doses.

- Do not eat fats with proteins. This means don't combine cream, butter, oil with meat, eggs, seafood, or nuts, for example. Too much fat can affect the gastric glands by reducing its ability to produce the right kinds of gastric juices and lower its performance by as much as 50%.

- Avoid combining acid fruits with proteins. This is to say oranges, tomatoes, lemons, pineapples, etc. should not be eaten with meat, eggs, cheese, or nuts. Sound pretty disgusting if you ask me, but many "gourmet" delicacies may inadvertently combine these unique ingredients. This combination is often seen on cheese platters served at special events. Acid fruits seriously affect protein digestion and leads to putrefaction. Putrefaction is the decomposition of organic matter, especially protein, by microorganisms, resulting in the production of foul-smelling matter.

- Don't eat melons with any other foods. Watermelon, muskmelon, honeydew melon, cantaloupe and other melons should always be eaten alone. This is more than likely due to the speed in which melons decompose.

TOTAL NUTRITION KITCHEN MAKEOVER™

If you follow these simple rules, you'll improve you're body's ability to assimilate nutrients, thereby feeling satisfied at every meal. You will no longer experience cravings or overeat, and weight loss will be simple and effortless.

FOOD COMBINING - VEGETABLES & GRAINS

Do Not Combine -
digests poorly together

Starches
All Grains
Bread
Brown & Wild Rice
Coconut
Corn
Lima Beans
Most Legumes
Parsnips
Pasta
Potatoes
Pumpkin
Whole Grain Cereals
Winter Squash
Yams

Proteins
All other bean products
Dairy**
Dried Peas & Beans
Flesh Foods**
Lentils
Nuts*
Seeds*
Soybean Analogs (fake meat)**
Sprouted Legumes

*Best soaked 24 hours in distilled water before use.

**Included for clarity ONLY. Not recommended.

Vegetables
Asparagus
Beets
Bok Choy
Broccoli
Cabbage
Carrots
Cauliflower
Celery
Cucumber
Eggplant
Kale
Kohlrabi
Leaf Lettuce & Endive
Okra
Onions
Parsley
Radish
Red, Yellow, Green Bell Peppers
Rutabaga
Snow Peas
Spinach
String Beans
Summer Squash
Sweet Potatoes
Turnips
Zucchini

Combine - digests well together

Combine - digests well together

Fresh
Vegetable Juice
Drink at least 30 minutes before a meal, and not with a meal. Barley Green is in the Vegetable Juice category.

Oils and Fats
Almonds
Avocados**
Butter*
Coconut
Flax Seed Oil
Olive Oil
Pecans
Pumpkin Seeds
Sunflower Seeds

A Note on Food Combining:
Various foods require different digestive juices and enzymes, and require different lengths of time for digestion. So, for optimal digestion and assimilation, it is best when foods are consumed in simple and compatible combinations. These food combining charts are included as a helpful guide, but are not absolute, and are not intended to be a set of unbending rules. Some recipes do violate ideal food combining guidelines.

*Use very sparingly. Never use margarine or other hydrogenated oils.

**Avocado is best mixed with green vegetables or sub-acid fruits.

MAIKA C. HENRY NORTHROP, ND

FOOD COMBINING - FRUITS

Do Not Combine - digests poorly together

Acid Fruits
Cranberries
Gooseberries
Grapefruit
Kiwi
Kumquat
Lemons*
Limes
Oranges
Pineapple
Pomegranates
Raspberries
Sour Plums
Strawberries
Tangelos
Tangerines
Tomatoes

*Lemons combine well with all plant foods and can be used to replace vinegar in recipes.

Sweet Fruits
Bananas
Dates
Figs
Muscat Grapes
Papaya
Persimmon
Prunes
Raisins
Thomspon Grapes
Other Dried Fruits

Sub-Acid Fruits
Apples
Apricots
Blackberries
Blueberries
Cherries
Guava
Kiwi
Mangos
Most Grapes
Nectarines
Papaya
Passion Fruit
Peaches
Pears
Plums

Combine - digests well together

Combine - digests well together

Melons
Eat melons alone or leave them alone, as they do not digest well with other food. However, any of the melons can be combined with each other.

Do Not Combine Fruits with Vegetables or Grains
An exception to this rule is that you may combine leaf lettuce or celery with fruits to help deal with the excessive sugar.

CHAPTER 16

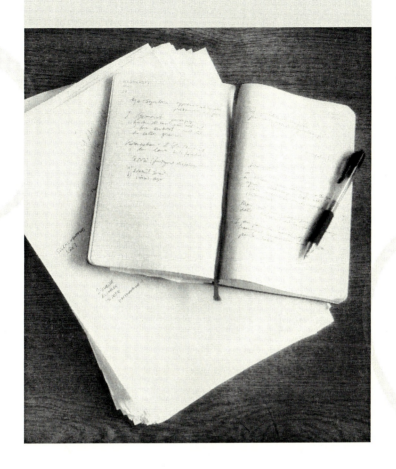

AUTHOR'S CLOSING STATEMENT

Now that we have come to the end of the kitchen makeover, let us recap some essentials.

We now know what diet is; it is what you eat. And a healthy diet is healthy eating.

We also know that healthy eating starts with healthy ingredients and healthy ways of preparation. We know enough not to be taken for a ride by those selling diets, an unhealthy lifestyle, chemically laden ingredients, liberating us from a boring chore—cooking.

We have learned that healthy eating and healthy cooking does not have to be a time-consuming bore. Armed with the right equipment, knowledge of ingredients, and a few recipes to start us off, we can create our own gourmet culture of healthy food. An exotic spice here, a flavoured herb there, a few drops of extra virgin tangy oil and vinegar, a quick shake and voila—what we have is a new and delicious creation to give flight to our senses and a boost to our health.

Be a discoverer, an inventor, a creative genius. Give fast foods a new meaning—healthy meals that don't take time and effort. And on this journey into the unknown, gather your family and friends. Your time in the kitchen is your time for rediscovering the roots of kinship, giving new meaning to your relationships with yourself and your near ones. Remember, the kitchen is not your domain alone. It is a place to invite others—family and friends—to share the excitement of discovery and inventiveness.

So let your creativity run free. Here's wishing you bon voyage on your new adventure—the newly rediscovered kitchen.

CHAPTER 17

SMART & HEALTHY KITCHEN RECIPES FOR LIFE

Remember, the key to a successful transition into the world of food preparation is to have all of your meals outlined for the week. Invest in a magnetized memo pad that you can mount on your refrigerator. Make sure you have all of the ingredients needed to carry out your meal plans for the week. Most importantly, combine and prepare all of your ingredients the night before and keep it in its designated pot or Ziploc bag in the refrigerator. If you are preparing for breakfast the night prior, feel free to start your automatic pot right before you retire. When you wake up the following morning, your house will be filled with the aroma of breakfast and you'll feel compelled to sit down as a family, even during a workweek. All that is required of you now is to pack your lunch and combine all of the ingredients in your pots for dinner. Presto, you have now become a domestic queen without spending an ounce of time in the kitchen. Who needs a personal chef—when they're highly overrated?

I've provided you with enough recipes to get you started, however I'm currently working on a more comprehensive recipe book as a follow-up to the Total Nutrition Kitchen Makeover™. If you would like more information about the products recommended in this book or would like access to more recipes, visit us on www.totalsensorywellness.com

TOTAL NUTRITION KITCHEN MAKEOVER™

CROCK-POT RECIPES

BREAKFAST
Maple Oatmeal w/ Dried Fruit and Apple Spice

1	cup	steel cut oats
1/2	cup	raisins or dried cherries or dried blueberries or dried sweetened cranberries (or a combination of)
1	teaspoon	apple pie spice
1	teaspoon	sea salt
1	tablespoon	extra virgin coconut oil
4	cups	water
2	tablespoons	pure maple syrup (plus extra for serving)

2 servings, 9 hours 10 minutes

Combine all the ingredients in a slow-cooker.
1. Cover and cook on LOW for 7-9 hours, or overnight.
2. Stir the oatmeal well and scoop into bowls.
3. Serve with organic coconut milk or regular milk with maple syrup.

Creamy Rice Porridge with Raisins

1	cup	medium grain rice, (or short-grain rice)
2	cups	water
1 1/2	cups	Thai organic coconut milk
1/2	teaspoon	sea salt
1/2	cup	raisins
1	teaspoon	nutmeg
1	teaspoon	cinnamon
1	teaspoon	organic vanilla extract

3 servings, 8 hours 10 minutes

1. Combine all the ingredients in a slow-cooker.
2. Cover and cook on LOW for 6-8 hours (or overnight) or until tender and creamy.
3. Stir the porridge well and serve straight from the pot with no embellishment.

Apple-Cinnamon Overnight Oatmeal

2	apples,	chopped and peeled

1	teaspoon	<u>cinnamon</u>
1/3	cup	<u>organic turbinado sugar</u>
2	cups	<u>old fashioned steel cut oats</u>
4	cups	<u>water</u>
1	pinch	<u>salt</u>

6-8 servings, 8 hours 10 minutes

1. Mix together the apples, cinnamon and turbinado sugar in bottom of Crock-Pot.

2. Sprinkle oats over apples, then pour in water and salt; DO NOT STIR!

3. Cook on LOW for 8-9 hours.

Hash brown Frittata Sensation

12		<u>eggs</u>
2	medium sized	<u>red russet potatoes</u> freshly grated
2	tablespoon	<u>olive oil</u>
1/2	cup	<u>red onions</u>, diced
1/2	cup s	hredded <u>raw cheddar cheese</u>
1	cup	<u>coconut milk</u>
1/2	teaspoon	<u>dry mustard</u>
		salt and pepper

10 servings, 8 hours 15 minutes

1. Layer the ingredients in your Crock-Pot in this order-.
2. 1/2 of the potatoes- on the bottom.
3. 1/2 of the onions.
4. 1/2 of the cheese.
5. Potatoes.
6. Onions.
7. Cheese.
8. Beat the eggs, coconut milk, olive oil, mustard, salt and pepper together. Pour this over the whole mixture. Cook on low for eight to ten hours.

LUNCH
Curried Vegetables

2	cups	vegetable or chicken stock
1	clove	garlic, crushed
1	teaspoon	turmeric

3/4	teaspoon	chili powder
1/2	teaspoon	ground ginger
1	teaspoon	coriander
1/2	teaspoon	celery chunks
1/2	teaspoon	zucchini strips
1/2	cup	green beans
1/2	cup	cauliflower pieces
1/2	cup	red and green pepper strips,
1/2	cup	sliced mushrooms
2		crushed and peeled tomatoes
1/2	cup	chopped shallots
2	teaspoon	sea salt

Servings, 6 to 8

1. Combine all of the ingredients in your Crock-Pot and cook on low for 8 to 10 hours.

2. Do not remove the lid during the cooking phase. Add additional crushed and peeled tomatoes last and allow to cook for an additional 10 minutes.

Caribbean-Style Black-Eyed Peas

1	cup	dried black-eyed peas
1	cube	vegetable bouillon cube
2	cloves	garlic, minced
1	onion,	medium, chopped
1/2	teaspoon	dried thyme
1/4	teaspoon	black pepper
1		habanero pepper, or less, seeds and stem removed, very finely minced (use rubber gloves)
1		Thai organic coconut milk, unsweetened (14 to 16 oz)
1/4	cup	water or broth
3	cups	hot cooked rice

1. Soak black-eyed peas overnight (adding sea vegetables to your water increases its mineral contents aiding digestibility); drain.

2. Combine black-eyed peas, vegetable bouillon cube, garlic, onion, thyme, pepper, minced habanero, coconut milk, and water in a slow-cooker.

3. Cover and cook on low 8 to 12 hours. Before serving, mix in rice (You can make the rice the night before and refrigerate; add to peas about

30 minutes before serving, turn to high, and heat through).

4. Serve with a side of salad and whole grain roll.

DINNER
Chili (For meat eaters and vegetarians)

1	lb	ground beef or substitute vegetable protein or add additional variety of beans such as pinto or chick peas for a vegetarian delight
2	red onions,	chopped
3	cloves garlic,	chopped
2	diced	tomatoes
3	tbsp	tomato sauce
2	tsp	sea salt
1	each	red, orange and yellow bell peppers, chopped
1	bunch	parsley, finely chopped
2	tbsp	agave syrup
1	tbsp	chili powder
1	tsp	ground cumin
1/2	tsp	dried oregano
	handful	red kidney beans
1/4	cup	water

8 servings

1. Cook ground beef or vegetable protein (add olive oil due to dryness) in heavy skillet until brown and drained. (For bean alternative: cook your beans in your Crock-Pot the day prior) Mix all ingredients and water in 3-4 quart slow-cooker. Cover and cook on low heat for 6-7 hours until vegetables are tender.

2. Uncover and cook for about 15 minutes, until slightly thickened.

Maika's Cajun Style White Beans & Rice

1	lb	Great northern white beans
1/2	cup	vegetable protein or cooked ground chicken
1/4	cup	chopped onions, red bell peppers
3	cloves	of garlic crushed
1	tsp	paprika
1	tsp	ground fenugreek
		sea salt and cracked peppercorn
1/4	cup	cooking oil (preferably olive oil)
1	bunch	finely chopped parsley

1. Let beans soak overnight in the refrigerator; drain. Put beans in Crock-Pot and cover with fresh water.

2. Put all ingredients except the parsley in slow-cooker with beans and their water; cover and cook on LOW for 8-10 hours.

3. When the beans are cooked remove enough liquid from the pot so that the beans can be felt 4 inches from the water line.

4. Take 1- 2 cups of the beans only and ½ cup of the juices from the pot and put it in a high powered blender until smooth and creamy.

5. Add gravy back into the Crock-Pot and stir until blended. Your beans should be hearty, rich and creamy.

6. Sprinkle the chopped parsley as garnishment or mix it in your beans.

Red Beans and Rice

1	lb.	small dried red beans, soaked overnight and drained
1	cup	chopped onion
3	cloves	garlic, minced
6	cups	hot cooked rice
1	cup	chopped green scallion onions
2	tsp	turmeric
2	tsp	paprika
		sea salt and white pepper
1		red dolce pepper finely chopped
1	tsp	ground coriander
1	tsp	ground cloves
1	handful	of finely chopped cilantro

1. In Crock-Pot, combine beans with all of the ingredients minus the rice and add 1 1/2 quarts water.

2. Cover and cook on LOW covered, 10 to 12 hours. When the beans are cooked, take 1 cup of the beans and ½ cup of the juices from the pot and put it in a high-powered blender until smooth and creamy.

3. Stir in the rice.

Roasted Lemon Pepper Chicken

1	thawed	small- to medium-size free range chicken
1/4	cup	lemon pepper seasoning

1	cup	water
1/2	1	lemon

1. Add 1 cup of water to your Crock-Pot, just enough to cover the bottom.

2. Place your chicken on a plate and squeeze lemon juice all over it. Sprinkle lemon pepper seasoning throughout your chicken. Be sure to cover your chicken with this incredible seasoning extremely well.

3. Sit your chicken upright into the center of the pot. Cover and cook on low for the next 8 – 9 hours.

Roasted Bone-Suckin' BBQ Chicken (a bit too spicy for children)

1	thawed	small to medium size free range chicken
1	cup	bone Suckin' sauce from whole foods Market
1	tbsp	garlic Season Salt
1	cup	water

1. Add 1 cup of water to your Crock-Pot, just enough to cover the bottom.
2. Place your chicken on a plate and sprinkle garlic season salt lightly throughout chicken.
3. Pour the Bone Suckin' sauce on your chicken and use a brush to spread it evenly throughout. Be sure to cover your chicken with this incredible sauce extremely well.
4. Sit your chicken upright into the center of the pot. Cover and cook on low for the next 8 – 9 hours.

RICE COOKER

Keep a few things in mind when cooking grains. Remember to always rinse grains thoroughly in cold water until the water turns clear. Get rid of the rinse water and then add the cooking water. When the rice cooker has completed its cooking cycle, be sure to test the grains to see if they are done. If the rice has a slightly chewy texture then it is ready. To increase digestibility of your grains (this is highly recommended if you have a history of digestive disorders) you may soak your grains overnight like you would beans. Finally, add a pinch of salt for every cup of dry grain you cook.

The following grains can be cooked in your rice cooker:

Brown Rice

<u>Quinoa</u> (pronounced keen' wah) is a sweet grain that is easy to digest and a great compliment to many dishes. It is light and has a pleasant texture.

<u>Oat Groats</u> are whole, unprocessed oats (Oatmeal is made from rolled oat groats).

<u>Barley</u> is loaded with more protein, iron, and calcium than wheat and combines well with other foods. It can be eaten at breakfast, lunch, and dinner.

<u>Amaranth</u> is a gluten-free alternative for those who are gluten sensitive. It's great combined with millet or brown rice or even as a thickener for sauces and stews. It can also be popped like corn as a great popcorn alternative.

<u>Kamut</u> is an ancient Egyptian wheat with a very chewy texture. It is great both cold and hot and makes great salad dishes.

<u>Millet</u> is considered one of the oldest grains. It is extremely aromatic and has a natural nutty flavor.

<u>Buckwheat</u> has a strong, robust flavor and is great in pilaf mixed with rice, vegetables, and other seasonings.

BREAKFAST

2	cups	long grain brown rice
1		Thai organic coconut milk w/o sugar (10 – 12 oz)
1		cinnamon stick
1	tbsp	extra virgin coconut oil
		a pinch of sea salt
1	tsp	organic vanilla extract
1/2	cup	chopped cashews
2	tbsp	agave syrup

1. Rinse rice thoroughly and drain.

2. In a saucepan heat coconut oil on medium heat. Add rice and cook, stirring constantly until it becomes opaque, about 3 minutes.

3. Transfer rice and all ingredients into rice cooker then stir in coconut

milk, water, nuts, cinnamon, vanilla extract, and salt. Bring to a boil.

4. Reduce heat to simmer, cover 20 minutes. Then remove from heat and let stand 5 more minutes. Remove cinnamon before serving.

LUNCH
Soy, millet and buckwheat casserole

1	cup	soy flour
1/2	cup	millet flour
1/2	cup	buckwheat flour
2 +	cups	water
5	tsp	olive oil
7	cloves	garlic
2	small	zucchini
1/2	med.	onion
		sea salt
4	sprigs	rosemary
	grated	tofu

1. Whisk together soy, millet, and buckwheat flour with water, salt, and two tablespoons of olive oil.

2. Grate the garlic with coarse grater and add.

3. Chop the zucchini and onions into tiny pieces and add to batter.

4. Chop rosemary into very fine bits and add. Mix all ingredients and cook on low in rice cooker for 3-4 hours.

DINNER
Rice cooker jambalaya

1½	cup	Your choice of uncooked whole grain rice (could be a medley of kamut, wild rice and brown rice)
2	tsp	Cajun seasoning
1		bell pepper
1	liter	chicken broth
1	lb	shrimp or crawfish
2	tsp	black pepper
1		olive oil
1	tsp	chili powder
1		onion
2	tsp	garlic powder

3	ribs	celery
1	tsp	accent
1	tsp	cayenne pepper

1. Combine all ingredients in the rice cooker and cook on regular cycle.

Rice and Peas

2	cups	long grain brown rice
4	cups	water
5	tsp	olive oil
2	tsp	sea salt
2	tsp	ground garlic
2	cups	frozen peas
2	tsp	cilantro

1. Combine all ingredients in the rice cooker and cook on regular cycle.

GEORGE FORMAN GRILL

BREAKFAST

Grilled Sweet Potatoes

1 – 2 medium yams or white sweet potatoes (the harder the better)

1. Peel the potatoes (optional) and cut them into approximately 1/4 inch strips (you'll find your favorite thickness after you cook them a few times).

2. Spread them across the grill and try not to overlap them too much. If you cut them a little thicker you'll fit more, but you don't want to make them too thick. You can fit about 1 1/4 pounds on a family-sized grill.

3. Cook them for 25 minutes. If you desire, you can flip them after about 20 minutes, but it's not necessary. These are absolutely delicious, and they go great with an omelet.

LUNCH

Grill Master Chicken Marinade

| 1/4 | cup | apple cider vinegar |
| 3 | tbsp | prepared coarse-ground mustard |

3	cloves	garlic, peeled and minced
1		lime, juiced
1/2		lemon, juiced
1/2	cup	raw cane sugar
1 1/2	tsp	sea salt
6	tbsp	olive oil
		ground black pepper to taste
6		boneless, skinless chicken breast halves

1. In a large, non-reactive container, thoroughly mix apple cider vinegar, whole grain mustard, garlic, lime juice, lemon juice, raw cane sugar, and sea salt. Whisk in olive oil and pepper.

2. Place chicken in the mixture. Cover, and marinate chicken in the refrigerator 8 hours, or overnight.

3. Spray the top and bottom of the George Foreman Grill with a no-stick olive oil spray then marinated chicken onto the grill—close and cook.

Grilled Eggplant and Tomato Salad

1	medium	eggplant
1		poblano pepper
3	cloves	of garlic, peeled
3	tbsp	olive oil
1	large	fresh garden tomato
1/4	cup	marinated kalamata olives, pitted and halved
2	sprigs	fresh oregano, chopped
3	sprigs	fresh basil, chopped
4	oz	fresh mozzarella, diced
		Sea salt to taste
		ground black pepper to taste

1. Slice the eggplant into half-inch rounds, brush each with olive oil on both sides, and sprinkle with sea salt.

2. Bring your grill to medium heat. Grill the whole pepper on all sides. Grill the eggplant slices over medium heat on both sides, until cooked all the way through, it takes about 5 minutes per side.

3. Oil the garlic cloves and wrap them in aluminum foil (before roasting) until soft and aromatic; it takes about 15 minutes. Leave the peppers, eggplant, and garlic to cool.

4. Dice the eggplant, pepper, and slice the tomato into wedges. Gently

toss the vegetables with the remaining ingredients, and season with pepper to taste.

DINNER
Roasted Eggplant and Garlic Bruschetta

3	med.	eggplants
7	cloves	cloves garlic, unpeeled
1	t	extra-virgin olive oil, plus more for drizzling
1/4	cup	coarsely chopped flat-leaf parsley
		kosher salt and freshly ground pepper
6		slices crusty whole-wheat bread
		thinly sliced onions and tomatoes
		assorted olives

20 minutes Serves 6

1. Heat the grill to medium heat and pierce eggplants with a fork. Place 6 garlic cloves on grill, drizzle with a few drops of oil. Grill eggplants and garlic for about 10 minutes, until eggplants are charred but soft. Remove from grill and cool. Halve the eggplant lengthwise and scrape out the flesh with a large spoon; discard skins.

2. Transfer eggplant to a blender. Squeeze the roasted garlic pulp from skins and add to eggplant along with one tablespoon of olive oil. Puree the mixture; add parsley and pulse. Transfer to a serving bowl; season with salt and pepper to taste.

3. Grill or toast bread, according to your taste. Peel remaining clove of raw garlic; cut in half and rub over bread, this gives it a delectable taste. Brush bread with oil and spoon eggplant spread on top of bread. Serve with onion, tomato slices, and olives as garnish.

Rosemary Shrimp Kabobs

8	oz.	fresh jumbo shrimp
		skewers
5	slices	turkey bacon, halved crosswise
3/4	cup	red, yellow, and/or green sweet pepper cut into 1-inch pieces
1	tbsp	freshly squeezed orange juice
4	cloves	of crushed garlic
1	tsp	snipped fresh rosemary
1 1/2	cup	hot cooked rice

3/4	cup	cooked black beans, rinsed and drained

1. Peel and de-vein shrimp, leaving tails intact. Rinse shrimp; pat dry with paper towels.

2. Wrap each shrimp in a half slice of turkey bacon. On 6-inch skewers, alternately thread shrimp and sweet pepper pieces.

3. In a small bowl combine crushed garlic, the orange juice, and rose mary. Brush over kabobs. Meanwhile, lightly grease the electric grill with olive oil or lightly coat with olive oil cooking spray.

4. Preheat grill. Place kabobs on the grill. If using a covered grill, close lid. Grill until shrimp turn opaque and bacon is crisp. (For a covered grill, allow 2-1/2 to 4 minutes. For an uncovered grill, allow 6 to 8 minutes, turning occasionally to cook evenly.)

5. In a medium saucepan stir together the cooked rice, beans, and re maining crushed garlic; heat through. Serve the shrimp and pepper skewers with rice mixture.

Makes 2 servings.

TOASTER OVEN

BREAKFAST
Wholesome Sandwich

1	loaf	whole wheat bread
1	med.	avocado, mashed
1	tsp	lemon juice
1	clove	garlic, minced
	Sea salt	
8	oz	cooked turkey meat or roasted red peppers for a vegetarian approach
2	med.	tomatoes, sliced
1/4	cup	chopped scallion
12	pitted	ripe olives
1	cup	shredded mozzarella cheese

1. Halve bread lengthwise and crosswise to make quarters. Place 2 bread pieces on oven pan of toaster oven. Repeat with remaining quarters of bread.

2. In a small bowl, mash avocado with lemon juice, salt, pepper and garlic. Spread 1/4 of mixture on toasted bread surface. Layer 1/4 of the turkey, cheese, tomato, and onion over the top of each.

3. Place 2 sandwiches on oven pan of toaster oven and brown until cheese is bubbly. Serve hot, garnished with olives.

LUNCH
Gardener's lasagna

6	cup	sliced zucchini
1/2	lb	ground turkey or roasted red peppers for a vegetarian approach
1	sm.	clove garlic, minced
1	cup	tomato sauce
	Sea salt	
1/4	tsp	dried oregano leaves
1/2	tsp	dried basil leaves
1	cup	curd cottage cheese
1	tsp	parsley flakes
1/4	cup	dry bread crumbs
1	cup	shredded mozzarella cheese

38 minutes cooking time

1. Use all ingredients listed above. Prepare as for oven. Bake at 350° for about 25 minutes.

2. Sprinkle with remaining half of mozzarella cheese and return to toaster-oven long enough to melt, about 3 minutes.

DINNER
Tropical chicken

4		boneless, skinless chicken breasts
8	oz	crushed pineapple
1/4	cup	home made mustard
1/4	cup	apple cider vinegar
2		soy sauce
2		raw cane sugar
1/8	tsp	ground ginger

4 servings, 45 minutes

1. Place chicken breasts in shallow dish.

2. Combine the remaining ingredients and pour over the chicken.

3. Bake at 350°F for about 35 to 45 minutes or until done.

VITAMIX JUICER

BREAKFAST
Extra Virgin Pina Colada

1		granny smith apple. cored, peeled and sliced
1	cup	fresh pineapple (remove the outer skin), cubed and cored
1	cup	water
2	tbsp	raw honey
1	cup	ice
8	oz.	Thai organic coconut milk

1. Add the water and ice first then the remaining ingredients. Begin blending the ingredients in your Vitamix juicer. Start on a low setting then work your way up to high, then to its maximum. This drink is sinfully good, but oh so healthy!

Blueberry Grape Juice Recipe

		handful of grapes
1	cup	blueberries, fresh
1/2	cup	water
1	cup	ice
1	tbsp	agave syrup

1. Add the water and ice first then the remaining ingredients. Begin blending the ingredients in your Vitamix juicer until nice and frothy, about a 5- 6 setting.

LUNCH
Pumpkin-millet Soup

1	med.	butternut squash (Japanese pumpkin)
6	cups	water
1	cup	dry millet
1-2	tsp	nutmeg
1/8	tsp	cayenne pepper
		your choice of vegetables
1	tsp	sea salt
1	tsp	agave syrup

1. Bring the water to boil in a pan, add millet, squash and other vegetables cook on low heat.

2. Before serving, puree the mixture in batches in vita mix juicer.

3. Add the nutmeg and pepper, and reheat for a few minutes.

DINNER
Fresh Broccoli Soup

2	tbsp	ghee (organic butter)
1		small onion cut in quarters
2	cups	broccoli, cut in big chunks
1 1/2	cups	chicken broth
1	cup	organic Thai coconut milk
1/4	tsp	sea salt
1/4	tsp	pepper

Servings, 3 ½ cups

1. In a medium saucepan over medium heat, sauté the onion in a touch of ghee.
2. Add chicken broth and broccoli to the onions. Bring to a boil, then reduce heat, and simmer about 10 minutes.
3. Place broccoli, onion, and broth in Vitamix juicer. Add coconut milk, sea salt, and pepper. Blend on high for 5 seconds.
4. Remove cover and check consistency. If desired, pour soup back into saucepan to reheat for a few minutes. Serve hot.

ELECTRIC PRESSURE-COOKER

LUNCH
Butter Beans in Mustard Sauce

500	gm	cooked butter beans
2	large	leeks
1	large	onion
2	cloves	garlic
2	tsp	ground mustard
2	tbsp	standard mustard
		organic Thai coconut milk
		season salt

cooking oil (preferably olive oil)

Serves 4-6

1. Fry the chopped onion and garlic in hot oil until pink and tender. Add chopped leeks, stir well, and cook for five minutes.

2. Add the beans, and two sorts of mustard, and then add the coconut milk slowly until a creamy consistency is achieved.

3. Add season salt to taste and serve with colorful vegetable and turmeric flavored rice.

DINNER

Homemade chili

1/2	lbs	lean ground chicken, or soaked kidney beans for a vegetarian approach
1/2		fresh chili
2	cloves	garlic, finely chopped
1/4	tsp	cinnamon
2	tsp.	ground cumin
1/2	tsp.	oregano
1/2	tsp.	black pepper
3	tbsp	chili powder
		cayenne pepper to taste for spicier chili
1 1/2	cups	water
1	large	onion, chopped
2	tbsp	olive oil

1. Heat pressure-cooker, sauté onion in olive oil. Add remaining ingredients. Close cooker securely.

2. Set pressure regulator to 15 lbs. Cook for 5 minutes. Remove and let pressure drop. Stir in chilies and return to a simmer for 10 minutes until heated through, stirring regularly.

3. Add water if too thick.

NATURAL STONEWARE CLAY

**Don't worry; you can cook a variety of dishes on your stoneware and it will not retain the flavor of the previous dish.

BREAKFAST
Buckwheat and fruit pancake

2	cups	buckwheat pancake mix
1	tsp	vanilla extract
2	tbsp	flax meal
1 3/4	cups	Thai organic coconut milk
2	eggs	slightly beaten
2	tbsp	ghee
1	cup	chopped, peeled pear, blueberries or sliced bananas

Makes up to 24 pancakes

1. In a mixing bowl, mix Buckwheat Pancake Mix, milk, eggs, oil, and vanilla. Stir until slightly lumpy. Mix in pear.

2. Heat oven to 400° Fahrenheit

3. Pour mixture on center of lightly buttered (with ghee) stoneware to approximately 4 inches in diameter. Pour four more times around the stoneware. You should be able to fit a total of 5 circular pancakes on the stone.

4. Cook until pancakes are a golden brown. Serve immediately or keep warm in a loosely covered ovenproof dish in a 200° F oven.

LUNCH
Panko Chicken

1-2	cups	Japanese panko breadcrumbs
1	tsp	sea salt
1	tsp	cracked peppercorn
2	tsp	dill weed
1	cup	vegannaise (whole foods Market)
1	lb.	chicken tenders

1. Put mayonnaise and breadcrumbs combined with remaining ingredients in two separate bowls. Dip chicken tenders into mayonnaise and then in breadcrumb mixture. Place on stoneware and bake at 350° until brown and cook thoroughly.

SNACKS
Chinese cabbage Salad

1	head	napa cabbage

1	bunch	minced green onions
1/3	cup	ghee
2	oz	homemade noodles
2	tbsp	sesame seeds
1/2	cup	slivered almonds
1/4	cup	apple cider vinegar
3/4	cup	vegetable oil

1. Shred the head of cabbage and combine the green onions in a large bowl, cover and refrigerate. Preheat oven to 350° F (175° C).

2. Melt the ghee in a pan and mix the noodles, sesame seeds and almonds into the pot. Spoon the mixture onto the round stoneware and bake in preheated oven, turning often to make sure they do not burn. When they are brown, remove.

3. In a saucepan, heat vinegar and oil. Bring the mixture to a boil, and allow to boil for another minute. Combine dressing, noodle mix, and cabbage immediately. Serve immediately.

DINNER

Broccoli Casserole

16	oz	chopped broccoli
1	tbsp	minced onion
1/4	tsp	sea salt
1/4	tsp	pepper
1/2	tsp	dry mustard
1/2	tsp	marjoram
½	tsp	savory
2	tbsp	ghee
2	tbsp	flour
1 1/2	cups	organic Thai coconut milk
1/2	cup	parmesan cheese
1	tsp	chicken bouillon

1. Melt ghee in a saucepan, add the flour and stir for one minute. Add coconut milk slowly and beat with a whisk while pouring.

2. Add chicken bouillon, spices, onion, and parmesan cheese to the pan. Mix with cooked broccoli and put in a pre-greased casserole stone ware dish. Bake for about 30 minutes at 350° F.

DESSERT

Crunchy Nutty Cookies

2	cups	ghee
4	cups	raw cane sugar
4	eggs	
8	teaspoons	vanilla extract
1	cup	finely chopped walnuts
1/2	cup	dried currents
2	teaspoons	baking soda
2	teaspoons	baking powder
2	teaspoon	sea salt
7	cups	whole grain pastry flour
32	ounces	unsweetened organic chocolate chips or carob chips (a great alternative to chocolate)

1. Mix the ghee with the raw cane sugar with an electric mixer until very fluffy.

2. Mix in the eggs and the vanilla.

3. Combine the dry ingredients and beat into the mixture. Slowly mix in the chocolate chips.

4. Drop by large spoonfuls onto the greased stoneware. Bake at 375° for 8 to 10 minutes, or 10 to 12 minutes for a crispier cookie.

BREAKFAST, LUNCH AND DINNER

Maika's Fabulous Organically Tantalizing Pizza

Even though you're making the dough from scratch, I promise you'll spend no more than 20 minutes in the kitchen. The dough is yeast-free, has a cookie-like consistency when cooked, and tastes great!

Pizza Dough

3	cups	whole wheat pastry flour
1	tbsp	flax meal
2	tsp	sea salt
1	tbsp	turbinado sugar
4	tbsp	olive oil
3	tbsp	rosemary
3	tbsp	baking powder
1 +/-	cup	water

1. Heat the oven to 350°. Combine all of the dry ingredients in a large bowl and mix thoroughly.

2. Create a whole in the center, and then add water and olive oil.

3. Fold mixture slowly with a large spoon until all ingredients have been blended and you have a workable dough.

4. Make sure your hands are clean and start kneading. The dough may appear slightly dry, that's o.k. it will still turn out great. Get a rolling pin and place you dough on the center of your stoneware and begin to form the dough until all edges of the stoneware has been covered. Set your dough aside.

Topping

½	cup +/-	organic spaghetti sauce, marinara sauce, or pizza sauce your choice of vegetables (i.e., mushrooms, red peppers, garlic, spinach, tomatoes, red onions, olives, capers, zucchini, etc.)
10	oz	organic mozzarella cheese and/or feta cheese
1	tbsp	dried pepper flakes
2	tsp	oregano
A pinch		season salt

1. Spread the sauce over your dough to approximately 1 inch from the edge.

2. Top with mozzarella cheese then your vegetables. I like to top my vegetables with feta cheese and olives.

3. Finally sprinkle some season salt, oregano and pepper flakes on top and place your pizza in the oven.

4. Cook for approximately 20 minutes or until slightly brown on top and the cheese is bubbling on the edge.

Mmmmm Good and healthy too!

References/Resources

Brown, J.E. "Ways of Knowing About Nutrition." Nutrition Now; Fourth Edition. (2005): Chapter 3, 1-20

Other information about Interacting with the Center for Food Safety and Applied Nutrition may be obtained at http://www.cfsan.fda.gov/

Food and Drug Administration/International Food Information Council Brochure (January 1992) Retrieved January 8, 2006 from http://www.cfsan.fda.gov/~lrd/foodaddi.html

Clayton College of Natural Health: Holistic Kitchen (2006) Retrieved January 22, 2006 from
http://www.ccnh.edu/holistichome/home_default.asp

Canadian Diabetes Association: Healthy eating is in store for you Retrieved February 3, 2006 from
http://www.healthyeatingisinstore.ca/labelling_resources.asp

Dietitians of Canada: Promoting Health through food and nutrition ((2006) Retrieved February 13, 2006 from
http://www.dieticians.ca/index.asp

Information about raw cultured vegetables using the fermenting pot can be retrieved from
http://bodyecology.com/aboutbed.php

The kitchen chick: The healing kitchen (2004) Retrieved March 10, 2006 from http://www.thehealingkitchen.ca/

Slow food USA: Living the Slow Life (2006) Retrieved for informational purposes only from
http://www.slowfoodusa.org/education/links.html

The Food Fit Company: Healthy Cooking (2006) Retrieved for informational purposes only from http://www.foodfit.com

Health Recipes, Inc. Retrieved for informational purposes only from
www.healthrecipes.com

Largeman, Francis A. Wild Blue (July 2006) Retrieved July 18, 2006 from
www.cnn.com/health

Mayo Foundation for Medical Education and Research: Disease and Condition Information (July 24, 2006) Retrieved July 28, 2006 from
www.mayoclinic.com

Elizabeth Bohorquez, RN, Personal Development Hypnotherapist, Sarasota Medical Center

Susan Burke, vice president of nutritional services for eDiet.com

Food and Drug Administration
http://www.FDA.gov

World Health Organization
http://www.WHO.org

National Diabetes Association
http://www.NDA.org

MEDICAL DISCLAIMER

If you were born in or currently reside in America, according to the FDA (Food and Drug Administration) it is important that you read the following medical disclaimer. Interestingly enough, all other countries are exempt from this law.

It is always best to consult with a physician/prescription drug provider before undergoing any major shift in your diet, especially if it completely alters your lifestyle and has the potential to dramatically improve your health.

The information given in this book is nothing more than opinions and/or suggestions, and is therefore protected under the First Amendment of the United States Constitution, which grants the right to discuss openly and freely all matters and viewpoints.

The viewpoints, opinions and/or suggestions found in this life promoting book should not be used for the diagnosis or treatment of any ailment. Nothing said, or hinted at being said, should be construed as medical advice.

The writer of these viewpoints cannot guarantee the accuracy or completeness of any information conveyed. All of the information contained within this book, as well as suggested websites, audio and other written material is provided with the understanding that the information and its providers shall not be responsible to any person or entity for any loss or damage caused, or alleged to have been caused, directly or indirectly by or from the information, ideas, or suggestions. Your participation with any of these ideas or edible items is solely done so at your own risk.

Finally, if you are currently taking any medications, please consult with your physician/prescription drug provider.

TOTAL NUTRITION KITCHEN MAKEOVER™

How your kitchen can help
save your life!